CUTTING
COLLEGE
COSTS

CUTTING COLLEGE COSTS

by
Bruce H. Donald

E. P. DUTTON, INC. / NEW YORK

Published in the United States by E. P. Dutton, Inc.,
2 Park Avenue, New York, N.Y. 10016

Library of Congress Cataloging in Publication Data

Donald, Bruce H.
  Cutting college costs.

  Bibliography: p. 237
    1. College costs—United States. I. Title.
LB2342.D66   1982   378'.38'0973   82-12792

ISBN: 0-525-48009-9

Published simultaneously in Canada by Clarke, Irwin & Company Limited, Toronto and Vancouver

10 9 8 7 6 5 4 3 2 1

First Edition

Contents

Preface and Acknowledgments   ix

I
THE FINANCIAL AID PICTURE

1. Considering College Costs   *3*
2. The Financial Aid Package   *10*
   Academics and Financial Aid   12
   Excessive Awards   14
   Major versus Minor Need   15
   Student Self-Help   19
3. Determining Eligibility   *26*
   Yearly Before-Tax Income of 0 to $9,999   29
   Yearly Before-Tax Income of $10,000 to $19,999   30
   Yearly Before-Tax Income of $20,000 to $29,999   31
   Yearly Before-Tax Income of $30,000 and Over   32
   Divorces and Separations   34
   College Aid Package   36
4. Improving Your Chances for Aid   *37*
   Evaluating Assets   38
   Reducing Income through Retirement Plans   47
   Bunching Your Children through College   50
   Parents as College Students   51
   The Independent Student   53
   Cheating   57
5. Accumulating Assets and Shifting Income
   to Minors   *60*
   The Uniform Gift to Minors Act   61
   The 2503-C Trust   63
   Estate Planning   63
   Tax Sheltered Annuities   65
   The Clifford Trust   65
   The Crown Loan   66

II
NEED-BASED FINANCIAL AID

6. The Programs 71
Federal Programs (Pell Grant, Guaranteed Student
Loan, Parent Loan, and Others) 71
State Programs (by State) 83
College Programs 107
Private Scholarships 107
National Merit Scholarship Program 110
Local Scholarships 111

7. How to Apply for Financial Aid 112
Federal Aid 112
State Aid 113
College Aid 115
Other Sources of Aid 115
Points to Remember in Completing
Applications 116

III
BEYOND FINANCIAL AID

8. College Comparison Shopping 123
State-Owned or State-Related Colleges and
Universities 126
Public Colleges of Other States 131
Less Expensive Colleges with Honors Programs 133
Cooperative Education 139
The Military Option 143
Foreign Study 157

9. No-Need Scholarships 163
Academic Scholarships 164
Athletic Scholarships 166

10. College Credit by Examination 171
Advanced Placement 171
CLEP 173
Nontraditional Education 179

11. Other Savings Strategies 184
Considering Geography 184
Commuting 187
Going Cheap, Graduating Expensive 189

Getting a Job with a College   191
Company-Sponsored Study   192
Buying a House   193
One-Time Tuition Payment   194

12. College and Financial-Aid Checklist   *197*
Tenth Grade   197
Eleventh Grade   198
Twelfth Grade   199

13. Best Buys   *201*
Twenty Best Buys   203
Forty Additional Good Buys   207

Appendix: List of No-Need Scholarships   *209*
Glossary   *233*
Bibliography   *237*

PREFACE AND ACKNOWLEDGMENTS

That college costs are frighteningly high and headed still higher is widely recognized. Any number of magazine and newspaper articles have thoroughly documented this unhappy situation, only to conclude by advising parents not to despair because financial aid is always a possibility. These two themes, spiraling costs and possible succor, have created our present college dilemma: college costs, especially at the more prestigious private colleges, are prohibitive unless a family is truly affluent or able to qualify for financial aid. Those families in the middle are caught between the well-known rock and hard place, too well-off to have someone else pick up the tab and too poor to ignore the financial consequences of their college choices.

While all families with college age or bound youngsters could benefit from reading *Cutting College Costs*, this book especially attempts to assist those middle-income families that have been ignored by traditional financial-aid literature. These families may not appear needy. In fact, they generally enjoy comfortable if not extravagant life-styles, and their incomes may range as high as $100,000. But educating children today is a traumatic experience for almost any family, especially if the family has to actually pay the prices that are listed.

This book is divided into three parts:

Part 1 describes how financial aid operates, allows readers to estimate whether they may qualify for aid, and suggests means by which families can increase their chances for aid and accumulate money to meet college expenses.

Part 2 explains how to apply for the various types of financial aid.

Part 3 proposes methods by which any family, no matter what its income, can save money on college expenses.

This book evolved from a booklet I wrote, as a guidance counselor, for the parents of students attending Haverford Senior High School in Havertown, Pennsylvania. When the booklet proved highly popular, I requested permission from the School District to expand and adapt it for a national audience. Permission was granted, and this book represents the improved work.

I wish to thank the School District of Haverford Township for granting me the right to publish this book and for providing the auspices under which my original booklet was first published. In particular, I want to express my appreciation to Dr. Gerald M. Hogan, Supervisor of Curriculum at Haverford, who first sensed the need for a book of this type.

Countless numbers of college financial-aid personnel whom I have badgered for information over the years also merit my appreciation. I have found them thoroughly professional people, invariably ready to answer every question and clear up any confusion even when their own institutions aren't involved. Two especially deserve thanks: Richard McQuillan of Ursinus College and William Parker of the Pennsylvania Higher Education Assistance Agency. Readers will soon discover that I am not an uncritical proponent of need-based aid. In spite of my tepid praise for financial-aid philosophy, my enthusiasm for the financial-aid community itself is unstinted. It is a hard-working and dedicated group.

My superb secretaries, Anne Pettit and Kathleen Ickes, also deserve my thanks. Without their ability to comprehend my hieroglyphics and their willingness to adapt to my time schedules I would have been lost.

Lastly, I wish to thank the students of Haverford Senior High and their parents for allowing me to observe how college costs and financial aid have touched their lives. Their insights and experiences have been invaluable.

Two notes concerning the wording of *Cutting College Costs:* Occasionally, an example of a hypothetical student is used as an illustration. Such a student will be referred to as *he*, merely to facilitate the readability of the material rather than to slight the other gender. Also, since it is parents who usually finance college students' educations, this book is directed toward them rather than their children.

Bruce H. Donald

I

The Financial-Aid Picture

1

CONSIDERING COLLEGE COSTS

Next to the purchase of a home, the largest single expenditure for many American families today is the cost of a college education. In fact, with total yearly expenses at some institutions totaling $13,000, it is no exaggeration to say that some families will actually spend more for their children's educations than they spent for their homes, and possibly much more. And perhaps this is as it should be if our society truly values excellence in higher education. Quality is expensive.

On the other hand, costs of this magnitude demand our full attention, no matter how worthwhile the education involved. Too much is at stake to risk making unwise choices or overlooking opportunities. Is the education offered by one college financially competitive with an education of similar quality obtainable elsewhere? Is the superior education offered by a "name" private college worth two or three times the price of the education offered by a less-renowned public college? What are the chances of obtaining financial aid based on need, "no-need" scholarships, or in some other way reducing the cost of attending a particular college? Is it possible for a student to earn a major part of his college expenses by working while attending college? Is it possible to delay college costs by borrowing money, possibly through low-interest loans? These questions barely scratch the surface. Families willing to take the time to familiarize themselves with college financing can frequently save thousands of dollars, sometimes simply by filling out the correct form and applying at the proper time.

Our present dilemma in financial aid stems from the 1960s, when the accessibility of higher education greatly expanded. Using the principle that federal aid should assist individuals rather than institutions, government aid increased spectacularly and enabled large numbers of needy students to attend college, many of them the first in their families to do so. Prior to this time most federal aid had assisted students less directly—for example, through the establishment of land-grant universities or through grants to improve the quality of science instruction.

Colleges expanded to meet the increased demand for their services resulting from both the higher percentage of students continuing their educations and the large number of college-age students that then existed. Many institutions that traditionally had catered only to the affluent suddenly found themselves with sizable percentages of lower-middle-class or poor students. This growth was welcome, but colleges also greatly appreciated the increased diversity that these atypical students had to offer.

As this was happening, during the 1970s a feeling emerged among many families that they were being shortchanged: that the wealthy could easily afford college, that the poor didn't pay for college, and that the middle class was either charged exorbitant prices or shut out altogether, especially from the more expensive institutions. Political pressure led eventually to passage of the Middle-Income Assistance Act of 1978. This Act both doubled the amount of money a family could earn while qualifying for federal aid and also established low-interest, government-guaranteed loans for all students regardless of family income.

Meanwhile, back at the Treasury, costs were rising. Higher education received $527 million in federal funds in 1947–48, $2.3 billion in 1964, and $13 billion in 1982. Growth such as this couldn't be overlooked by a conservative administration committed to reducing governmental expenses, especially when the military was earmarked for a buildup. Consequently, a decrease was proposed and angry cries arose.

What can we conclude? First, it would appear that over the next few years there will be a constant battle between Washington and powerful vested interests over aid to higher education. Since neither is likely to achieve its objectives fully, compromises will prevail. Although much aid will remain available, federal aid will become harder to obtain. What is available will pay a smaller percentage of college expenses. Moreover, colleges will be hard pressed until they can adjust themselves and their admissions patterns to a lower level of governmental support for student aid. When a college alters its admissions pattern, it takes four years before it is fully reflected throughout its student body.

Second, federal aid, the dominant economic force in higher education, will continue to be dispensed largely on a person-by-person basis. While this is undoubtedly the most expensive and cumbersome method for distributing money ever devised, aid to individuals rather than institutions has become firmly entrenched in higher education; its proponents proclaim that, whatever its shortcomings, philosophically it represents the fairest solution to the problem.

To understand the problem posed by college costs, perhaps we should begin by examining expenses at some of the more popular colleges and universities. The following table represents room, board, and tuition charges for the 1982–83 school year.

COLLEGE EXPENSES 1982–83

	Tuition and Fees	Room and Board	Total	Additional Tuition for Out-of-State Residents
Arizona State University	$ 710	$2,320	$ 3,030	$2,540
Beloit College	6,586	2,100	8,686	
Bowdoin College	7,665	2,880	10,545	
Brown University	8,430	3,135	11,565	
Clemson University	1,400	1,815	3,215	1,438
College of William and Mary	1,574	2,682	4,256	2,434
Cornell University	7,950	3,050	11,000	
Macalester College	6,280	2,180	8,460	
Middlebury College (Comprehensive fee)			10,800	
Oberlin College	7,755	2,855	10,610	
Reed College	7,160	2,630	9,790	
Rice University	3,700	3,200	6,900	
Smith College	7,750	3,100	10,850	
Stanford University	8,220	3,423	11,643	
Tulane University	5,934	2,810	8,740	
University of Iowa	1,040	2,020	3,060	1,440
University of Notre Dame	5,950	2,000	7,950	

	Tuition and Fees	Room and Board	Total	Additional Tuition for Out-of-State Residents
University of Oklahoma at Norman	721	2,076	2,797	1,150
University of Rochester	7,080	3,152	10,232	
Ursinus College	5,005	2,300	7,305	
Vanderbilt University	6,100	2,925	9,025	
Villanova University	5,300	3,120	8,420	
Washington University	7,179	3,237	10,416	
Western Kentucky University at Bowling Green	626	1,996	2,622	1,154
Yale University	8,190	3,600	11,790	

A few things should be kept in mind. First, total costs for a college student are considerably higher than simply room, board, and tuition. There are books and supplies, lab fees, spending money, transportation costs, clothes, fraternity or sorority dues, and dental and medical bills, to name just a few. Many students will want to have a car on campus, too. Frequently there will be more exotic requests, such as a semester in Washington, D.C., a junior year abroad, or a spring vacation in Ft. Lauderdale or Bermuda. It's hard to say what other expenses will arise, but you can be certain that they will. I can think of one biology major who wanted to accompany her class to the Galapagos Islands in order to observe their distinctive flora and fauna. In view of her major, it struck her as a reasonable request.

Next, we should remember that costs are not static. They rise yearly, and since the costs listed here represent 1982–83, a student in college beyond that school year will pay more, possibly much more. Recently, increases of 10 percent or more per year have been common. For example, at Vanderbilt University, tuition costs have risen from $3,950 in 1978–79 to $4,260 in 1979–80, $4,700 in 1980–81, $5,300 in 1981–82, and $6.100 in 1982–83.

Obviously, educations also differ drastically in cost. For instance, four years at a public college might cost only about one-third to one-half as much as the same four years at a private one. At even the cheapest, however, if more than one child in a family attends college and/or one or more decide to attend graduate school (graduate tuition is higher than undergraduate, and most medical schools are astronomically expensive) some impressive totals can be tabulated. Moreover, if we were to incorporate expensive colleges into our calculations, our totals could go through the roof. It becomes child's play to reach $100,000 through this kind of analysis. In fact, when inflation is considered, that $100,000 could easily be spent putting just one child through an Ivy League university plus graduate school.

These figures appear frightening, but in fact relatively few families actually attain these levels; the main reason that the totals are cited is to illustrate a potential rather than to predict an outcome. In the first place, a great many families today receive financial aid toward college expenses. On many campuses 30 to 50 percent of the students are receiving aid, and on some campuses it is 80 or 90 percent. Obviously, we're not discussing something reserved for a few prodigies and athletes. Even in these days of relative austerity much financial aid remains available, substantially more than was offered prior to the Middle-Income Assistance Act of 1978.

In the second place, more affluent, middle-class families who fail to qualify for aid frequently cut corners, generally by having their children attend public rather than private colleges or having them live at home and commute. As this book will demonstrate, students have many alternatives other than going public or commuting. These are merely the first that spring to mind. Informed families have many options.

This brings us to the crucial question: How can parents purchase the most appropriate education for their child at the lowest possible price? Both of these factors, suitability *and* price, are important. Finding the proper college isn't much of a challenge, and neither is finding an inexpensive one. Getting a good, inexpensive education is the trick.

To solve this problem satisfactorily we must begin by discussing financial aid. This is the economic litmus test of higher education. Those who are able to qualify for aid, either immediately or after some financial cosmetics that will be discussed, have one series of options. Those who, like an overweight wrestler, just can't qualify no matter how hard they try have a different set of options. The next chapter will explain how financial aid operates.

2

THE FINANCIAL-AID PACKAGE

Let's take a look at the mechanics of financial aid. When a family applies for aid, an analysis is made of the parents' income, their assets, the number of children, the number of children in college at the same time, unusual medical expenses, the age of the parents (to determine nearness to retirement), unusual family obligations such as dependent grandparents: in short, everything related to a family's financial health. A figure is then arrived at that this family is expected to pay toward college expenses. The difference between this figure and the cost of the college the student wishes to attend represents the family's *financial need*. *Financial aid* is the means of meeting this financial need. The following examples illustrate how this may work:

College	Cost of Attendance	Expected Family Contribution	Financial Need	Financial Aid Award
A	$12,000	$5,000	$7,000	$7,000
B	8,000	5,000	3,000	3,000
C	4,000	5,000	0	0

Financial aid is normally awarded as part of a package: part grant (a grant is a gift; it need not be repaid), part loan, and part work (colleges normally expect students on aid to earn some of the money they need by working summers or on campus). If the need is $4,500, a possible package might be $2,500 in grant (parts of which might come from several sources: federal, state, private scholarship, college scholarship), $1,000 in loan, and $1,000 for an on-campus and/or summer job. These proportions could vary depending upon the wealth of the college and desirability of the student. Thus, an outstanding halfback with the same need might receive a $4,500 grant, or a $3,500 grant and a $1,000 easy job.

AN EARLY WARNING

Each year that the student is in college the application process must be repeated, and the amount of aid granted fluctuates to reflect changes in the family's ability to pay. Theoretically, this paragraph should end here, but it appears that some colleges have been more liberal in their financial-aid awards to freshmen than to returning students. Their reasoning seems to be based on the idea that it is crucial to entice freshmen to their institution and that most of these students probably won't leave if they are gradually cut back after the first year. Since counselors receive no direct feedback from colleges concerning financial-aid awards, merely word of mouth from counselees and parents, this is something which can't really be documented. No doubt there are those that do and those that don't cut back aid, and while it would be nice to pinpoint which are which, without direct feedback, such as counselors receive in regard to college acceptances or rejections, I'd merely be guessing. You might keep it in mind as a point to ponder if you really start looking at a college. Don't be afraid to ask questions.

ACADEMICS AND FINANCIAL AID

The most common misconception concerning financial aid is that only "smart" students can qualify. There are certain prizes awarded by colleges (see appendix 1) for academic excellence, as well as special incentive programs, such as athletic scholarships (discussed in chapter 9, "No-Need Scholarships"), but generally speaking the academic competence of a student has absolutely nothing to do with the computation of his financial need. Once the financial need is determined, it is possible that academics play some part, but not nearly to the extent commonly believed. Private scholarship plans often combine need with other qualities, such as class standing, good citizenship, and academic aspirations of the applicant, as the criteria they use for selection. Moreover, with insufficient funds available to satisfy everyone's need, colleges may discriminate, deciding to meet one candidate's need because they really want him, but not another candidate's because in the final analysis they're not really that concerned about whether he enrolls. Most state and all federal monies, however, are distributed without considering academics. It is irrelevant if an applicant is first in his class and has 1600 on the SAT, or is last with 400. Even for marginal or weak students, my experience has been that many colleges do come through with money if the need is there. For financial aid, the first criterion is need, not grades.

Recently Derek C. Bok, president of Harvard University, suggested that student eligibility for Pell Grants, one of the major types of federal aid, should be tied to SAT scores and high school rankings as well as to financial need. He noted that students in the lowest quarter of their high school class with SAT scores of 700 or less have only a 30 percent probability of finishing their course of study. Moreover, 40 percent of all students entering college fail to receive a degree.

Perhaps the government will include scholastic aptitude as one of the aid criteria in the future, but as yet there is no sign of it. And if there is movement in this direction, Washington will face a battle because many educators are bitterly opposed to awarding aid on any other basis than financial need. They point out that SAT scores are related to family income (the higher the income, the higher the SAT score), and certain minorities have not scored well because of low incomes and bad schools. In addition, certain areas of the country perform better on the SAT than other areas, and politicians are sensitive to anything that might adversely affect their states. While including SAT scores as a criterion for aid would seem logical from the educational and economic viewpoints, critics question its fairness.

Clearly, then, the word *scholarship* is usually misapplied, which is frustrating to counselors. Many colleges that use this term award money solely on the basis of need. Nevertheless, the students who receive these "scholarships" frequently have their pictures in local papers and their names read at graduation ceremonies, while their classmates with far superior credentials receive no mention whatsoever. What causes the confusion is that there are so many kinds of scholarships: some based purely on need, some based partly on need and partly on academics, and very few based solely on scholarship. Since it's so hard to distinguish among them, and *scholarship* has such a pleasant ring, all scholarships are generally viewed as academic honors, which is what creates such confusion in the minds of parents. They just can't believe that their little genius might not get a cent, or, for that matter, that their little underachiever might qualify for a bucketful.

EXCESSIVE AWARDS

If a student is awarded more money than he needs to attend college, the college readjusts its financial-aid package so that the student can't make money. For instance, if a student with a financial need of $3,000 has been awarded a $1,000 grant, a $1,000 loan, and $1,000 employment by a college, and then wins a company scholarship of $1,000, the college will reduce its package by $1,000. They may reduce his loan to $500 and have him working less and earning $500. Consequently, this student's revised package would be a $2,000 grant, a $500 loan, and $500 work. Usually colleges want to make trying for outside scholarships worthwhile, so they rarely just withdraw their own grants when students obtain grants from other sources. Even if they do, it normally isn't dollar for dollar, so it's helpful to get aid from as many sources as possible rather than relying on the college for everything. This is especially true today, when so many colleges are short of funds. A student may be able to save himself considerable debt by locating private scholarships and substituting them for the loans he would otherwise have to take.

MAJOR VERSUS MINOR NEED

Something else to remember is that you'll stand a much better chance of obtaining grants (easily the most attractive part of a financial-aid package) if your need is substantial. Families with little need—$1,500, let's say—usually have trouble qualifying for college grants. Sometimes the state or federal government will contribute something if family income falls within the proper limits, but colleges tend to ignore such trivial need whenever their money is involved. Their philosophy is that the family that qualifies for $1,500 in aid receives it when their child is asked to borrow $1,000 and earn $500. The family doesn't have to pay this $1,500; their child does. To top it off, when they publish their statistics regarding financial aid, most colleges include that student.

Students with major need have tended to do quite well in regard to financial aid in recent years. As a counselor I've observed instances in which it has been perfectly logical for a student from a low-income family to attend an expensive college but made no sense at all for another from a more affluent background.

Recently, however, economic problems in financial aid have surfaced, principally because of the cutbacks in federal aid. According to a chart published by the College Scholarship Service, federal aid of all types accounted for 78 percent of all student aid in 1980–81. College aid and other private programs provided only 16 percent, and state aid 6 percent. Since this dominant federal aid will not be as plentiful as before, many colleges will face some painful choices:

Reject Some Needy Students. Colleges can take financial need into consideration when admitting students. Wesleyan University, for instance, after years of "aid-blind" admissions, will now include aid as one of its admissions criteria. A well-endowed university, Wesleyan will continue to accept and award aid to many students, though not as many as before. And as a recent article in the *New York Times* explained, citing Virginia B. Smith, president of Vassar College, "Private colleges and universities such as Vassar could probably continue to subsidize the 20 percent or so of students they have carried on scholarships before the 1960s, but that, given the cuts now being enacted in federal aid, there was no way that the current level of more than 40 percent could be sustained."

Accept Needy Students but Offer No Aid. Colleges can continue "aid-blind" admissions but award no college aid (as opposed to federal or state) to certain aid candidates. The colleges that practice this decide which students they really want and make these aid awards as attractive as possible. Losing a high percentage of the rest is acceptable, since these places can easily be filled by students able to afford the school. This practice is commonly regarded as accepting through admissions and rejecting through financial aid.

Sometimes this produces surprising results. One prestige college that recently switched to this practice found that most of their "accept/no-aid" students came to them anyway. Evidently some families are in better financial shape or are willing to endure more hardships than people realize.

Remember that this practice involves only college

money. All colleges are happy to see students receive aid from other sources, and financial-aid officers are even responsible for dispensing much of the federal aid.

Accept and Fully Aid Needy Students, but Pay the Price. Colleges can continue to meet students' needs and replace federal dollars with their own, basically through increased tuition. Idealistic aid officers favor both "aid-blind" admissions and financial aid fully meeting the needs of all accepted students, a combination that theoretically would permit any student to attend the college of his choice.

The chief drawback is that whenever a college raises its tuition, a smaller percentage of the student body actually pays it. Let me illustrate, again with Wesleyan. Wesleyan found that whenever tuition was raised, aid automatically had to be increased dollar for dollar, since any student who couldn't afford, say, $10,000, would surely need $1,000 more if the cost became $11,000. Therefore, with 40 percent of the student body already receiving aid, any increase in tuition would be paid for by, at the very most, 60 percent of the students. Moreover, as tuition rose, that 60 percent would become 55 percent, 50 percent, etc., as more students qualified for aid. Every $100 increase in tuition, which theoretically should have yielded an additional $260,000, actually produced only $156,000. In short, 60 percent of the students were bearing the burden of Wesleyan's inflation.

Therefore, each increase in tuition must be greater than would theoretically be necessary to meet rising costs. The extra aid expenditure that accompanies each tuition hike is one of the reasons college tuition has been rising so rapidly. At least 50 percent of the aid awarded by colleges is entirely unfunded and merely subtracts from college income. It's a myth that college financial aid is financed by endowments.

In fairness, I must also point out that, unlike Wesleyan, many colleges have difficulty attracting sufficient students. Therefore, these think of financial aid the way airlines think of filling the last few seats on a plane. Since whatever they obtain from or for these students is more than they would receive if they couldn't replace them, these colleges argue that they are maximizing their net income by awarding financial aid. For them financial aid is a revenue producer, not consumer.

One college official, for instance, confided to me that his institution could lower its tuition by 10 percent *if* it could fill all of its seats without offering financial aid to some pupils. Since it's questionable whether it could reach full enrollment even with a lower tuition and since this financial aid does help to keep the student body more heterogeneous, this college continues to operate as usual.

While all colleges are increasingly learning to appreciate applicants capable of financing their own expenses, these three options chiefly involve those colleges that have meaningful aid programs of their own. Take a look at the aid distributed at one private junior college, as shown in the table on page 19.

This junior college itself contributed $18,000, or only about 1 percent of the total aid received by its student body. Unfortunately, this situation is not unusual. Many colleges aren't remotely similar to a Wesleyan or a Vassar, and they couldn't care less whether a student applies for aid.

Pell grants (federal)	$244,692
Supplemental Educational Opportunity Grants (federal)	123,305
National Direct Student Loan (federal)	203,761
College work study program (federal)	93,750
State grants	210,101
State Guaranteed Student Loans	547,184
Student grants from other states	192,937
Other outside grants	20,000
College-sponsored grants:	
College-sponsored grant in aid	15,000
Memorial scholarship	1,000
Alumnae scholarships	2,000
Total aid	$1,653,730

STUDENT SELF-HELP

Until recently, college aid officers hated to saddle a student with more than $2,000 to $3,000 of self-help (loan and job) because students can earn only so much, and they didn't like seeing a young person heavily in debt. Recently this has begun to change. Because of financial pressures many colleges, especially expensive ones, are beginning to look to the student for $4,000 or more. One expensive university, for instance, now expects any student with need to borrow $2,500 per year through a Guaranteed Student Loan and to earn $1,800 more from summer and campus-based jobs. Consequently, unless a family's need exceeds $4,300 a year, this university doesn't begin to consider grants. Think of that—$4,300 a year from just the student! That's more than the total yearly cost of many public colleges and universities. And lots of students at public institutions are receiving aid, too.

For students with severe need, another school expects $4,800 a year in self-help ($2,500 Guaranteed Student Loan, $1,500 National Direct Student Loan, and $800 in work). These figures may vary. If a student can earn more than $800, his loan will be less than $4,000. This $4,800 of self-help applies only to those with severe need, though, so many students in better circumstances have a lower self-help expectation and are able to qualify more easily for at least something in grants.

The philosophy of the college is a factor. Let's say a college has $200,000 of its own funds to distribute. Should it award $4,000 each to 50 students, $1,000 each to 200 students, or some combination of the two? Students with severe need can quickly soak up all of the available aid. Colleges reach different conclusions on this question. One states, "Awards are made first to those with the greatest need." Another writes, "Although the parent contribution is based on the national system, each institution can make its own adjustments. Because the college has a special concern for middle-income families, home equity is viewed conservatively in relation to present high market values." No doubt both of these institutions will make every attempt to dispense their aid as fairly as possible. But there's a difference in attitude, isn't there?

Examine financial-aid literature critically. Superficially, most of it sounds the same, but some does communicate an extra message. Occasionally it helps to chat with the school's financial aid officer, too. Some philosophies exist in fact but not in print.

If you do hope to qualify for aid from a college, it's wise to analyze which colleges can afford extensive aid programs of their own to supplement federal and state aid. According to the United States Department of Education, the following 100 institutions were the most heavily endowed in 1979, holding at that time more than two-thirds of all college endowments. Since there were 3,152 colleges, universities, and branch campuses in the United States in 1979–80, that doesn't leave much for the rest.

ENDOWMENT FUNDS OF 100 LARGE INSTITUTIONS OF HIGHER EDUCATION, FISCAL YEAR 1979

Institutions	Market value of endowment (in thousands of dollars)
United States (all institutions)	$18,158,634
100 institutions with the largest amounts	12,785,411
University of Texas at Austin	1,159,388
Harvard University (Mass.)	1,145,692
Yale University (Conn.)	585,414
Stanford University (Calif.)	516,234
Princeton University (N.J.)	474,329
Massachusetts Institute of Technology	380,698
University of Rochester (N.Y.)	327,206
Columbia University, Main Division (N.Y.)	322,830
University of Chicago (Ill.)	311,191

Institutions	Market value of endowment (in thousands of dollars)
Rice University (Tex.)	282,025
Northwestern University (Ill.)	277,855
New York University	271,727
Washington University (Mo.)	226,468
Johns Hopkins University (Md.)	202,830
Rockefeller University (N.Y.)	201,794
Dartmouth College (N.H.)	189,524
California Institute of Technology	174,727
Emory University (Ga.)	168,171
Cornell University Endowed Colleges (N.Y.)	158,451
University of Notre Dame (Ind.)	137,526
Vanderbilt University (Tenn.)	137,489
Wellesley College (Mass.)	133,741
University of Southern California	130,254
University of Pennsylvania	127,342
University of Michigan, Ann Arbor	121,166
Cornell University Statutory Colleges (N.Y.)	120,999
Case Western Reserve University (Ohio)	118,245
University of Virginia, Main Campus	117,232
Carnegie-Mellon University (Pa.)	112,799
University of Delaware	109,264
Brown University (R.I.)	106,600
Wesleyan University (Conn.)	104,756
Duke University (N.C.)	103,459

Institutions	Market value of endowment (in thousands of dollars)
Smith College (Mass.)	97,692
University of California, Los Angeles	96,607
University of Minnesota, Minneapolis-Saint Paul	92,805
University of Pittsburgh, Main Campus (Pa.)	91,615
University of Minnesota, Mayo Graduate School of Medicine	91,085
Oberlin College (Ohio)	89,296
University of California, Berkeley	88,909
University of Cincinnati, Main Campus (Ohio)	88,016
Rensselaer Polytechnic Institute (N.Y.)	87,396
Williams College (Mass.)	84,703
Amherst College (Mass.)	77,321
Berea College (Ky.)	76,633
Southern Methodist University (Tex.)	76,435
Swarthmore College (Pa.)	75,290
Vassar College (N.Y.)	74,821
Trinity University (Tex.)	73,268
University of Richmond (Va.)	71,154
Princeton Theological Seminary (N.J.)	68,686
Ohio State University, Main Campus	66,167
Baylor University (Tex.)	62,773
University of Washington	62,426
University of Wisconsin, Madison	61.140

Institutions	Market value of endowment (in thousands of dollars)
Brandeis University (Mass.)	59,632
Wake Forest University (N.C.)	58,983
Rochester Institute of Technology (N.Y.)	57,795
Lehigh University (Pa.)	56,940
Lafayette College (Pa.)	54,340
Texas Christian University	53,650
Wabash College (Ind.)	52,850
Mount Holyoke College (Mass.)	52,532
University of California, Davis	52,345
Loyola University in New Orleans (La.)	52,000
Tulane University of Louisiana	51,234
Middlebury College (Vt.)	50,084
Saint Louis University, Main Campus (Mo.)	49,825
Butler University (Ind.)	49,004
Carleton College (Minn.)	48,890
Syracuse University, Main Campus (N.Y.)	48,741
Pomona College (Calif.)	47,777
Thomas Jefferson University (Pa.)	46,335
Bryn Mawr College (Pa.)	46,052
Bowdoin College (Me.)	43,949
Stevens Institute of Technology (N.J.)	43,491
Rush University (Ill.)	43,137
University of California, Santa Barbara	43,107
Grinnell College (Iowa)	40,846
Loyola University of Chicago (Ill.)	40,764

Institutions	Market value of endowment (in thousands of dollars)
Jarvis Christian College (Tex.)	39,737
State University of New York at Buffalo, Main Campus	39,693
Hamilton College (N.Y.)	39,289
Trinity College (Conn.)	38,931
City University of New York, Mount Sinai School of Medicine (N.Y.)	38,078
Boston University (Mass.)	37,852
Agnes Scott College (Ga.)	37,795
Cooper Union (N.Y.)	37,561
University of North Carolina at Chapel Hill	37,088
Colgate University (N.Y.)	35,873
Whitman College (Wash.)	35,861
Purdue University, Main Campus (Ind.)	35,659
University of Miami (Fla.)	35,600
Worcester Polytechnic Institute (Mass.)	35,226
Georgetown University (D.C.)	35,081
Bucknell University (Pa.)	34,919
Tufts University (Mass.)	34,276
Northeastern University (Mass.)	34,164
Yeshiva University (N.Y.)	33,952
Union College (N.Y.)	32,812

SOURCE: U.S. Department of Education, National Center for Education Statistics, special tabulations from *Financial Statistics of Institutions of Higher Education, Fiscal Year 1979.*

3

DETERMINING ELIGIBILITY

Now that we understand the operation of financial aid, let's tackle the big question: Can you qualify? The following Parents' Expected Contribution Chart for 1982–83, from the College Scholarship Service, is one good means of estimating what you will be expected to pay. Although this chart stops at assets of only $40,000, it can be extended by adding $570 for every $10,000 in assets above this amount.

Remember that this calculation is merely an educated guess and that actual analysis will probably differ. Moreover, individual colleges may or may not accept the recommendation of the advisory service. When the College Scholarship Service or the American College Testing Service submits an evaluation, it's merely an opinion, and no college is bound by it. The colleges, not CSS or ACT, hand out the money.

Since CSS and ACT coordinate their efforts, theoretically which one conducts the analysis should have no bearing upon the result. Even so, most colleges are adjusted to one or the other, so they usually make a point of specifying which they want. The problem is that CSS and ACT use different formats. Typically, when a report arrives at a college, a clerical worker keypunches the information for the computer. If the wrong report arrives, this worker may incorrectly enter information or simply set it aside because he doesn't know how to handle it. Sometimes it slips to the bottom of the stack and just sits. One way or another, the wrong report can foul things up.

Another method of estimating what you will be expected to pay is to request a copy of "Meeting College Costs," which is published by CSS, or the "Financial Aid Tabloid," published by ACT. Both are free, updated yearly, and available through high schools.

Families willing to invest a little money can utilize the "Early Financial Aid Planning Service" offered by CSS. For $7 CSS will return a completely confidential analysis of how they would have treated your financial situation if your application had been an actual request for aid. Theoretically, therefore, families can determine years ahead of time what the future may hold.

Exciting though this may sound, many financial-aid officers lack enthusiasm for it. They fear that some families will read the results, decide that they don't qualify for aid, and then fail to apply when it comes time for their children to attend college. These officers suspect that some of these families actually would qualify later on if they applied, because the need analysis may change and college costs will continue to escalate, and they wonder whether too much knowledge too early is really a benefit.

It's possible that some of these fears have substance, but I would still opt for families learning as much as possible about financial aid and other economic aspects of financing college as early as possible. There's so much money that can be saved by knowledgeable families that it makes little sense to leave them in ignorance because some of them might misuse the knowledge.

PARENTS' EXPECTED CONTRIBUTION

Net assets:	$10,000				$20,000			
Family size:	3	4	5	6	3	4	5	6
Income before taxes:								
$8,000	$ 0	$ 0	$ 0	$ 0	$ 0	$ 0	$ 0	$ 0
12,000	0	0	0	0	0	0	0	0
16,000	520	80	0	0	620	200	0	0
20,000	1,120	690	280	0	1,190	780	390	0
24,000	1,730	1,260	860	400	1,790	1,330	940	510
28,000	2,460	1,880	1,410	960	2,500	1,940	1,480	1,040
32,000	3,380	2,650	2,080	1,540	3,380	2,690	2,130	1,610
36,000	4,420	3,640	2,930	2,250	4,420	3,640	2,960	2,300
40,000	5,390	4,630	3,920	3,100	5,390	4,630	3,920	3,120
44,000	6,290	5,530	4,830	4,020	6,290	5,530	4,830	4,020
48,000	7,190	6,440	5,730	4,920	7,190	6,440	5,730	4,920
52,000	8,010	7,280	6,600	5,820	8,010	7,280	6,600	5,820
56,000	8,800	8,070	7,390	6,610	8,800	8,070	7,390	6,610
60,000	9,590	8,860	8,180	7,400	9,590	8,860	8,180	7,400

Nevertheless, parents should keep in mind that they must reevaluate their financial planning for college every year in light of their changing economic circumstances and in regard to the newest practices involving financial aid. Even if you have applied for aid previously and been rejected, it pays to keep trying. A rejection is for that year, not for always.

Applications for this service are available from Early Financial Aid Planning Service, College Scholarship Service, Box 2843, Princeton, New Jersey 08541; phone (609) 734-3941.

Net assets:	$30,000				$40,000			
Family size:	3	4	5	6	3	4	5	6
Income before taxes:								
$8,000	$ 0	$ 0	$ 0	$ 0	$ 0	$ 0	$ 0	$ 0
12,000	150	0	0	0	410	0	0	0
16,000	750	350	0	0	1,010	610	230	0
20,000	1,300	900	530	100	1,590	1,170	790	360
24,000	1,910	1,440	1,060	640	2,260	1,740	1,330	910
28,000	2,610	2,050	1,600	1,160	3,060	2,430	1,920	1,430
32,000	3,490	2,790	2,240	1,720	4,060	3,270	2,650	2,020
36,000	4,530	3,750	3,070	2,420	5,100	4,310	3,580	2,840
40,000	5,500	4,740	4,030	3,230	6,060	5,300	4,590	3,760
44,000	6,400	5,640	4,940	4,130	6,960	6,210	5,500	4,690
48,000	7,300	6,540	5,840	5,030	7,860	7,110	6,400	5,590
52,000	8,110	7,380	6,710	5,930	8,680	7,950	7,270	6,490
56,000	8,900	8,170	7,500	6,720	9,470	8,740	8,060	7,280
60,000	9,690	8,960	8,290	7,510	10,260	9,530	8,850	8,070

NOTE: The figures shown are parents' contributions, assuming the older parent, age forty-five, employed; the other parent not employed; income only from employment; no unusual circumstances; standard deductions on U.S. income tax; and one child in college.

SOURCE: Reprinted by permission from *The College Cost Book*, copyright 1981 by College Entrance Examination Board, New York.

Finally, here is a very rough guide based on what I have found tends to happen with each income group.

YEARLY BEFORE-TAX INCOME OF 0 TO $9,999

Families in this range should easily qualify for financial aid, frequently maximum aid, from all sources.

Typically, most of these families will have an expected contribution of zero.

The children, on the other hand, will face certain problems. First, they may be forced to borrow money for college, sometimes substantial amounts. For instance, I can recall two children from one family that had a zero expected contribution. The first went to a state college, and the combination of federal and state awards plus work were enough to finance his education. The second elected to attend a more expensive private college, and part of his aid package was a sizable loan, which absolutely enraged him. He couldn't understand why he'd have to borrow when his brother didn't. A second problem confronting these students is that colleges may think twice about accepting them, since they will qualify for so much aid.

Students from these families would be wise to apply for every possible scholarship, not just the governmental and college sponsored ones. The vast majority of private scholarship programs use need as the main element, and if a family's circumstances are such that one scholarship committee will award money to them, chances are excellent that a second, third, and fourth will feel the same way. If the student mentioned above had been energetic, he probably could have collected awards from private sources, and his loan might not have been necessary.

YEARLY BEFORE-TAX INCOME OF $10,000 TO $19,999

Most families in this range have a good chance of qualifying for aid. The number of children in a family, the number in college simultaneously, and family assets are all important items, though, so some families with equivalent earnings could be far apart in their expected contributions. Some could have a zero expected contribution while others might have to pay $2,000. Most of these families will easily qualify for federal and probably state money, although they may or may not receive the maximum amounts. Private scholarships are also well worth pursuing for this income bracket. Insofar as college acceptances are concerned, many of these students will face the same problems as the preceding group since their need for college aid could be great.

YEARLY BEFORE-TAX INCOME OF $20,000 TO $29,999

Families falling into this bracket sometimes qualify for substantial aid, and sometimes they don't. The $20,000-plus area is marginal. To begin with, most state and federal programs have cutoffs in the mid-twenties (this will vary depending on many factors: family size, assets, college costs, etc.), so some families will fail to qualify for governmental aid. If they do qualify, frequently it will not be for a maximum grant.

Private scholarships are also harder to come by, since these families look almost affluent when compared to families with incomes of $8,000 or $13,000. I have seen families in this income range qualify for private scholarships, however, so the possibility should not be overlooked. Try to determine how keen the competition is for a scholarship before you apply. Any scholarship that offers only one or two awards and has about thirty applicants a year probably isn't worth pursuing for families in this bracket. A few of those thirty are bound to appear poor in comparison to a family with say, a $25,000 income. But some scholarships are less eagerly pursued and offer more awards. Frequently a scholarship that offers fifty awards doesn't receive fifty times as many applicants as one offering one award. Try to sound out someone knowledgeable about an award before you apply. Sometimes you can quickly discover that you aren't a logical candidate and concentrate your efforts instead on more realistic possibilities.

Generally, the $20,000-plus area is a hard one to predict. These families aren't really poor, but under the right circumstances they can establish substantial need. Two families can each have $25,000 incomes, and one may make out royally while the other receives nothing.

Some ironies can develop. One Pennsylvania family I know has two children in college, one a state college in Pennsylvania and the other an expensive private college in New York. The child attending the Pennsylvania college can't receive a state grant since the cost of the college is too low. The child attending the New York college could easily qualify for a Pennsylvania grant, but since New York doesn't allow its aid to leave the state, Pennsylvania won't allow its aid to flow to any New York college either. Consequently, this family receives no state aid.

YEARLY BEFORE-TAX INCOME OF $30,000 AND OVER

Basically, these families are beyond the range of federal and state grants, although in the past some managed to slip in if their incomes weren't much over $30,000. Guaranteed student loans are still a possibility, however. Private scholarships, too, are hard to come by unless they don't receive many applications or show the applicant preferential treatment.

College financial aid is probably the likeliest source of assistance for these families. Expensive private colleges frequently extend aid to families with incomes substantially over $30,000, and aid to families with incomes greater than $50,000 is not unheard of. Take a look at the following chart prepared by the University of the Pacific, showing the relationship between family income for dependent students and financial aid received at UOP, without considering factors such as family assets, business or farm assets, family size, or the number of family members in college.

Average Financial-Aid Awards by Family Income Level Awarded 1981–82

Family Income	Percent Awarded	Number of Recipients	Average Award	Range of Awards
$1–10,000	93%	121	$8,653	$1,625–13,327
10,001–17,500	95%	222	8,235	1,200–12,727
17,501–25,000	93%	252	7,302	550–13,227
25,001–30,000	88%	210	6,887	100–14,001
30,001–35,000	87%	166	6,236	800–10,951
35,001–40,000	83%	122	5,328	250–8,379
40,001–45,000	72%	64	4,797	250–7,801
45,001–50,000	68%	36	4,671	850–8,327
above 50,000	29%	34	3,949	100–8,101
Totals	83%	1,227	$6,892	$100–14,001

That's an impressive aid program, and remember that this is the University of the Pacific, not Harvard. Much of the aid received by the lower income brackets is obviously governmental, but the university is still very much involved, especially at the high end. Much aid is available for families with substantial incomes *if* an expensive college with a sizable endowment is involved. Otherwise, frankly, families with $40,000 or $50,000 incomes don't have much hope of obtaining need-based aid.

DIVORCES AND SEPARATIONS

This is an important consideration that could affect aid awards. Unusual family relationships are the bane of financial-aid officers. On the one hand, they want to be fair to the child, who has already suffered from the upheaval, and on the other, they want to be sure that parents aren't evading their responsibilities. Some years ago, for instance, some expensive colleges discovered that a few parents were faking divorces so that only the wife's income would be examined. But what do you do when a student's father walks out of the house to get a pack of cigarettes and simply disappears? Often the college director of financial aid has to make a subjective decision based on the particular situation. If you have problems, see him. Also, if a decision goes against you, don't be afraid to ask the director to review your case. Sometimes mistakes are made; perhaps he'll be more receptive to your need if the particulars are explained to him in greater detail.

In spite of the subjectivity involved, there are some general guidelines concerning unusual family relationships:

1. Only natural or adoptive parents, not foster parents or other persons providing support, are considered to be parents when a student applies for financial aid. A legal guardian appointed by a court may in certain cases be considered a parent.
2. If the natural or adoptive parents are separated or divorced, the parent is considered to be the one with whom the student has lived for the greater portion of the last twelve months. Generally, the other parent's income and assets are not included in the evaluation of a family's ability to finance the education, although some colleges may still try to go after the absent parent, unless he or she remarried.
3. If the student did not live with either parent, or lived with each for an equal number of days, for financial-aid purposes list whichever parent provided the greater support.
4. If a parent has remarried, a stepparent's financial information must be included if the student lived or will live with the stepparent for more than six weeks in the last or next calendar year *or* did or will receive more than $750 in support from the stepparent in the last or next calendar year.

Some family relationships become very complicated. If the above guidelines leave you in a quandary, make an appointment to see the financial-aid officer of the college of your choice. If that college is too far away, pick a nearby college. My experience has been that financial-aid officers are happy to answer questions whether or not their institution is involved.

COLLEGE AID PACKAGE

Before we proceed to the next chapter, which will offer advice on how to improve your chances for aid, we should examine what a college financial-aid package represents. Let's say that in March a college sends you an aid package like this:

$1,200	Estimated Pell Grant
800	Estimated State Grant
1,500	College Grant
2,500	Guaranteed Student Loan
1,000	College Work-Study
2,000	Parent Contribution
$9,000	Estimated College Expenses

Take a close look at those first two entries. They contain the important word *estimated*. The problem is that both federal and state governments usually fail to appropriate the money necessary to fund these awards until the last minute, sometimes not until after the students are already in college. As a result, colleges "estimate" what students will receive.

Sometimes these estimates are incorrect because the legislators balk at appropriating sufficient funds. Consequently, if the Pell Grant is reduced from $1,200 to $1,000 and the State Grant from $800 to $600, someone has to come up with an extra $400. Some colleges are considerate and wealthy enough to pick up that extra $400, but quite a few won't. A student and his family have to be prepared to compensate if what they think they'll receive fails to materialize in full.

4

IMPROVING YOUR CHANCES FOR AID

Much like an income-tax guide, this section will analyze various economic considerations regarding financial aid and suggest means for improving your odds.

Let's begin by understanding precisely where we are. Financial aid is a kind of welfare system. Most people don't associate the two, since there is a stigma attached to welfare that is completely missing from financial aid. Except for that, there is no difference. Financial aid and welfare are both motivated by the same kind of idealism and plagued by the same kinds of problems.

No aspersion is intended toward people who receive either form of assistance. Welfare is necessary for disadvantaged people; and insofar as financial aid is concerned, a strong case could be made against the government for allowing tuitions to reach such ridiculous levels that most American families need aid. It's one thing to establish a system to assist special cases, but it's quite another when runaway tuition creates a need to accommodate everyone. I can recall one student who came to my office almost in tears because every scholarship she investigated was based on need. "Everyone thinks we're wealthy because my father is a doctor, but we aren't," she complained. When even our most highly paid professional people encounter difficulty meeting tuition bills for their children, there is something fundamentally wrong with our system of financing higher education.

My sole purpose for establishing the similarity between financial aid and welfare is to orient the reader to the job at hand. When money is distributed on the basis of need, it becomes logical for a family to take certain actions that would make no economic sense under normal circumstances. Perhaps some of the thinking in this section will strike the reader as negative. If so, please keep in mind that I didn't create the game; I'm merely analyzing how to win at it. No matter how addicted you are to the Puritan ethic, this is not the time for it.

EVALUATING ASSETS

One of the chief ingredients of any financial-aid analysis will be assets, since families with assets are assumed to be in a stronger economic position than families without them. Financial-aid officers make no moral judgments about what is declared. They simply accept what is. If a family with a $30,000 income is flat broke, so be it. That family will fare better than a $30,000 family that has accumulated assets.

Mechanically, it works this way. First, a portion of family assets are protected so that a family isn't forced to impoverish itself to educate the children. Candidly, this figure is rather meager. For the average family in which the older working parent is in his fifties we're talking about $35,000 to $40,000. Younger parents would have less of an allowance; and older ones, because of their nearness to retirement, receive a larger allowance, up to $55,400 if they are sixty-five or older. The totals for one-parent families are less, about $27,000 to $31,000 for a parent in his fifties.

Consequently, if a family has $70,000 in assets and a $40,000 asset-protection allowance, $30,000 of that original $70,000 is considered discretionary net worth. Not all of this must be spent on education, however. That $30,000 is next multiplied by 12 percent, and the resulting $3,600 is added to the family's income. This adjusted income figure determines how much aid, if any, the family will receive.

HOME EQUITY

The primary asset of most families is the equity they've built up in their homes. This figure is calculated by subtracting the remainder of the mortgage from the current market value of the property. Frequently this is a problem because people either lack a realistic idea of their home's true value or choose to understate its worth. Consequently, family estimations are taken with a heavy dose of salt by financial-aid people.

What they put more faith in is the original price the family paid for the property and the year they purchased it, information that the family must also supply. These are objective facts about which most families are truthful. Using this hard data, colleges will compute what they feel is a realistic market value for the property, normally assuming a 7 percent rate of inflation for the 1970s and a 4 percent rate for the 1960s. These rates could be higher if they feel the property is located in a section of the country that has experienced more rapid real estate inflation. If this estimate is close to the family's, usually they'll accept the family's figures. Otherwise, they'll substitute their own—without notifying the family.

A family with a home that for some reason has failed to keep pace with inflation, perhaps because it's located in a declining neighborhood, would be wise to explain this situation to the college financial-aid officer.

OTHER ASSETS

In addition to home equity, all equity in any other real estate or business, plus all investments, such as stocks, bonds, and checking and savings accounts, must be listed. Investment collectibles such as coins, stamps, gold, silver, etc., also should be included, though occasionally this area is murky. What is a stamp collection worth? Using listed values of stamps doesn't mean that the owner could actually receive these prices. What about valuable paintings? Are they investments or just part of the decor, like fine furniture? Consumer items such as home furnishings, cars, television sets, and stereos are not included.

Currently, tax-sheltered retirement plans such as Keogh plans or IRAs are also exempt, but this is now under review. It appears that by 1983–84 the net asset values of these accounts will be requested by at least the College Scholarship Service and the American College Testing Service. Many expensive private colleges feel that families with assets in these plans are better off than those without them, so they are urging their inclusion. Indications are that the federal government will probably retain, at least temporarily, the tax-sheltered exemption insofar as its aid is concerned.

Another contemplated change involves the wording of the aid applications. Currently, it isn't sufficiently specific, so many people with bank certificates or tax-free bonds neglect to include them either because of ignorance or an actual desire to defraud. Tax-free bonds, especially, have been a problem. While some people may continue to cheat, the proposed wording would force them to lie. Feigning ignorance will not be as easy in the future.

Realistically, financial-aid officers have to rely heavily upon the basic honesty of most applicants insofar as assets are concerned. Otherwise the system would break down. While incomes are easily verifiable, assets, unless they reveal their presence on a tax form, can be understated or hidden entirely. Some people would prefer to see them completely eliminated from the need-analysis system. At one point the federal government moved somewhat in this direction and abolished home equity for federal aid awards for 1982–83, but it was reinstated a few months later.

DEBT IN RELATION TO ASSETS

Some people mistakenly believe that they will qualify for more aid if they go further into debt. Normally, this isn't true. One man, for instance, sold his home, which was almost mortgage-free, and purchased a newer and much more expensive one simply because his children were reaching college age. He thought that going from $5,000 in debt to $60,000 in debt would increase his financial aid. The financial-aid people, however, indicate that this isn't true since his equity remained the same. On the other hand, if he had borrowed an additional $55,000 and had not put it into real estate but instead frittered it away on consumer items, presumably he would indeed have qualified for more aid. However, I don't recommend this as a means of increasing aid awards.

THE STUDENT'S ASSETS

A key aspect of our asset evaluation must be the student's assets. Any assets he possesses are considered available to meet college expenses, and they are largely confiscated during his college years. For instance, if a student has assets of $4,000, about a third is listed as available to meet the first year's college expenses, so about $1,333 will be so designated that year, before the student's parents' assets are even considered. Each year this process repeats itself on the basis of what the student has left, so there isn't much left by graduation. This process is considerably stiffer than if the $4,000 belonged to his parents.

A fascinating aspect of this child and family asset situation concerns gifts to minors. A sophisticated method for a middle-class family to save money for college expenses is to give money to their children so that the assets may grow tax free (since most minors don't earn enough to pay taxes). When a family does this, however, under present methods of analysis they greatly hinder their opportunities for financial aid. On the other hand, if they fail to utilize this opportunity to avoid taxes, there is no guarantee that they'll qualify for aid when it comes time to apply anyway. This question and various financial strategies are discussed in chapter 5, "Asset Accumulation and Shifting Income to Minors."

Another intriguing situation arises when a student

decides to delay college for a year in order to save money toward college. Assuming that such a student comes from a family that could qualify for aid and that he is honest enough to declare his savings when he does apply for college aid, he won't accomplish much, since whatever money he saved he'd probably receive anyway. His savings merely reduce his aid, especially what he might hope to receive as an outright grant.

Once I pointed out these inequities to a financial-aid officer. After conceding that there was an element of unfairness, he observed that parents always put down zero for their children's assets anyway. Even assuming that he was exaggerating, I did perceive the situation in a new light.

INVESTMENTS

When a family has an income-producing investment, their chances for aid are hindered in two ways: first, because the investment income raises the family's income; second, because the investment exists simply as an asset. Your equity in your home, on the other hand, hurts in only one way: as an asset. It produces no income. This treatment of investments and income is similar to double taxation. In fact, if we also consider the effects of income taxes on the income and of possible personal property taxes on the asset, it could even be thought of as triple or quadruple taxation.

Nice though it is to have assets, they do create certain problems. Perhaps assets could be decreased for a constructive purpose or the income traded for greater asset growth or delayed until a more favorable time.

First, assuming that it's possible, consider paying off your mortgage. This would leave you with the same assets but less income. The advantage is the possible income-tax savings and the increased chances for aid. The main disadvantage is the loss of interest expense as an income-tax deduction. The key element here is your mortgage rate. If it's low, this wouldn't make sense; if it's high, it could be a good idea.

Second, before your children enter college you should screen your securities for capital gains and losses. Gains should be taken prior to their entering college or delayed until they leave, but losses should be saved until they enter. Perhaps you'll need a handy loss to offset a gain you have to take while they're there.

Bonds can be particularly valuable insofar as capital gains and losses are concerned. Since interest rates have soared in recent years, bonds have dropped in value and many investors are sitting with substantial unrealized losses. (Question: How does someone acquire a $1 million portfolio of bonds? Answer: First, he starts with $2 million.)

If this applies to you, consider selling your bonds when you want a loss and switching these funds to a deep-discount bond that matures just after your children have graduated. Such a bond would sell well below face value and pay moderate income while your children are in college, and after they graduate, you'll realize a capital gain as the bond matures. Moreover, that capital gain will be taxed at a lower rate than if it had been ordinary income.

Another possibility is to switch into investments that are more growth- than income-oriented. Stocks paying high dividends or investments such as bank certificates or money-market funds can be traded for growth-oriented stocks or mutual funds. Some investors may hesitate to leave the security of high-paying, conservative investments for the vicissitudes of the stock market. If you lack experience in investing or the temperament to accept uncertainty, your hesitation is probably warranted.

Incidentally, if you do decide to switch to a mutual fund, select a "no load fund." Unlike a "load" fund, a no load requires no salesman's commission. That's the only difference, though salesmen will claim otherwise. In late August or early September *Forbes* magazine does an annual survey of mutual funds that I have found very useful.

There are numerous strategies for shifting income from a time when it isn't welcome to a more favorable time. For instance, interest earned from funds in money markets and savings accounts is taxed at year's end. If these funds were shifted to investments such as treasury bills, bank certificates, or corporate bonds that would not mature or pay interest until the following calendar year, income would be shifted from the current to the next year. For instance, let's say a bond has coupons dated January 1 and July 1. If you were to buy that bond on July 2, you would not receive income from it until January.

There are many more strategies for shifting or reducing reported income, and some are more complex than those I have described—real estate or oil and gas leasing, for instance. But these require considerable financial experience. Readers who wish to delve more deeply should contact a brokerage firm. Canny investors can usually select when they wish to accept income.

Perhaps some of my readers by now are asking

themselves how sophisticated financial maneuvering such as this has relevance to a financial-aid book. Well, remember that some families with incomes as high as $50,000 or $60,000 can occasionally qualify for aid at expensive colleges if they have unusual circumstances, such as many children, two or three in college. Also, widows frequently possess substantial assets from life-insurance policies and little or no earned income. While it's admittedly advantageous to be penniless when applying for aid, an oath of poverty is no absolute requirement.

A final consideration involving investments is the relationship between the size of an investment and the amount of the investment income. Let's say a family lists $20,000 in investments and $5,000 of investment income. Colleges commonly suspect that the $20,000 declaration is understated, since a 25 percent return is remarkably good. If you find that your financial acumen has produced an especially favorable financial result, it would be wise to contact the college financial-aid officer before he does something you might regret.

EARNED INCOME

For most people, earned income is an even more crucial area of concern than investments and investment income. After all, most people applying for financial aid lack sizable investments, and parents can't quit their jobs in order to qualify for aid. The gain in aid would be more than offset by the loss in earning power. There are some people, of course, who join the underground economy to avoid taxes and increase aid (absolutely illegal on both counts, and not recommended). There are others, salesmen or businessmen perhaps, who can occasionally control when they receive payment for their services. But most families haven't had many options. Here are a few suggestions.

REDUCING INCOME THROUGH RETIREMENT PLANS

By far the best means of decreasing income has been a tax-sheltered retirement plan. Unfortunately, it appears that its appeal from a financial-aid standpoint will be lessened somewhat in the future. The three most common types of tax-sheltered plans are Individual Retirement Accounts (IRAs), Keogh Plans, and 403b Plans.

Under the new tax law, every worker has the right to contribute up to $2,000 of his earnings to an IRA, even if he is also contributing to another tax-sheltered plan. Families with two working spouses can establish an IRA for each and contribute up to $2,000 for each. Families with a nonworking spouse can open a spousal IRA account and contribute as much as a combined total of $2,250. Distributions from the plan cannot begin without penalty until age 59½ and must begin no later than 70½; the only exceptions are for permanent disability or death.

Keogh Plans permit a self-employed worker to contribute 15 percent of his net earnings up to a maximum of $15,000 a year. Retirement ages, penalty, and exceptions are the same as for IRAs.

The 403b Plans, which constitute tax-sheltered annuities for teachers plus some other workers in nonprofit situations, permit a worker to have up to 20 percent of his income deducted from his salary for the annuity. Moreover, if he hasn't taken advantage of this option in previous years, he is permitted to recapture part of his unexercised shelters up to a maximum of $3,200 a year.

Since IRAs can be combined with both Keogh and 403b plans, substantial amounts can be deducted from incomes. Families investing money in tax-sheltered plans have been able to decrease their incomes and taxes, increase their chances for aid, and greatly increase their rate of saving as these tax-sheltered assets grow unimpeded by taxation. Colleges may try to reduce some of this attraction, but for now, and at least in the near future:

Money that is deducted from earnings reduces family income and taxes. It appears that both the federal government and colleges will continue to accept this lower income total in determining financial aid.

Asset values of tax-sheltered accounts are entirely free of taxation. While it seems likely that the federal government will continue to exclude these assets from aid calculations, colleges will probably start to insist on their inclusion. If so, this will be reflected in future copies of the FAF of the College Board and the FFS of the American College Testing Service.

Assets that exist in tax shelters produce income that is untaxed. This income will almost certainly continue to be excluded from all aid calculations.

The net result is that most of the advantages of these investment vehicles should remain, even if some adverse action is taken. Let's examine an extreme situation to see how much of an effect tax shelters can have. If a teacher earning $24,000 a year hasn't contributed to a 403b plan previously or has contributed less than the maximum, potentially he could contribute 20 percent of his salary ($4,800) plus $3,200 to make up for previous years. In addition, he can contribute $2,000 to an IRA. What might happen is shown below:

$24,000	earnings before shelters
− 10,000	maximum contribution to shelters
14,000	taxable income
+ 1,200	addition to income based on $10,000 in assets
$15,200	adjusted family income for aid from college sources

When one reflects upon how rapidly assets can grow in a tax-free environment (at 10 percent interest, assets double in a little more than seven years, quadruple in less than fifteen years), it's foolish not to take advantage of this option, especially when you also decrease taxes on your earned income and expand your opportunities for financial aid. The major drawback to the tax-sheltered retirement strategy is that many families that are seeking aid live from paycheck to paycheck. Asking them to voluntarily take a cut in pay is like asking them to jump off the Brooklyn Bridge.

Nevertheless, the advantages are so great that the possibility should be weighed. Perhaps some assets could be set aside prior to the college years and used to supplement the decreased income. Also, do you really need a vacation home? Do you have a stamp or coin collection that could be cashed in? Could you borrow money? Can you tighten your belt and pass up a new car? A vacation? Clothes that are in style? Eating out?

The answers to these questions will determine whether you can save money on taxes, receive more financial aid, and build up a tidy nest egg for retirement. It's your choice.

BUNCHING YOUR CHILDREN THROUGH COLLEGE

Here's another legal way to greatly improve your chances for aid, but it's probably going to sound as though I'm recommending the Brooklyn Bridge again. If you have several children to send to college, send as many as possible at the same time. Send them through in convoys. If you have two in a row, either have the first wait for the second to start or have the second finish high school a year early. If you have three in a row, the first could wait a year and the third graduate early. The reason is that families with more than one in college at the same time aren't asked to pay any more for two or three in college than for one, assuming they can qualify for financial aid.

Let's observe how this works. Take a family that is expected to pay $7,000 a year for one child in college. Since this family actually has two in college, it is expected to pay up to $3,500 per child. Child A is attending a community college, and since his total costs are less than $3,500, the family will qualify for no aid for him. Child B is attending a private college costing $8,500 a year; the family will need $5,000 ($8,500 − $3,500) for this child and can hope to receive $5,000 in aid.

Having children in college simultaneously can make an enormous difference in total costs for families who can establish need. Let's say a family can pay $7,000 a year according to need analysis and has three children to put through expensive colleges. If each child started college when the other finished, the family would have to spend $84,000 (12 years × $7,000), but if they went through college simultane-

ously, the cost would be only $28,000 (4 years ×
$7,000).

With several children in college at the same time,
even families that normally wouldn't receive aid
could qualify. A family that is expected to pay $14,000
could still qualify for aid if it had two or three in
college simultaneously at expensive colleges.

PARENTS AS COLLEGE STUDENTS

The College Scholarship Service and the American
College Testing Service consider every member of a
family (including parents) who is enrolled at a college
half-time or more as a full-time college student. Unfortunately, some colleges don't accept this analysis,
which could cause a vast difference in aid offers to a
family that falls into this category.

For instance, one family was delighted when CSS
included the mother, who was attending the local
community college part-time, as a student. The
daughter, who had applied to Penn, expected to qualify for substantial aid. Penn, however, viewed the
situation differently. In the first place, they try to
avoid including parents as students; and since the
costs of the mother's part-time attendance at the
community college were negligible in comparison to
what the daughter's would be at Penn, they decided
that this was a one-student family. Second, since the
mother had accepted a job during the year, they
assumed that she would continue working all of the
following year and based their earnings figure for this
family on future anticipated earnings rather than the
previous year's actual earning. This type of analysis,
which colleges with extensive aid programs com-

monly perform to adjust the evaluations of the College Board or American College Testing Service, considerably weakened the "need" of the daughter.

Out of curiosity I sampled several other colleges to see how they would have handled this situation. Basically, most of them agreed with Penn, and those that didn't lacked significant aid of their own. The most interesting response was from a university that has aid available, though not to the same extent as Penn. Its financial-aid officers agreed with Penn but said that they weren't positive they would have noticed the situation. Frequently, because of time pressures and the great numbers of aid applications, they simply accept the evaluation of the College Scholarship Service. If someone from their financial aid staff had chanced upon that application and analyzed it, however, they probably would have treated it as Penn did.

Financial-aid officers deal with thousands of applications, questions from parents, missing or incorrect figures from applications, changes of legislation. Each application for aid frequently requires examination from several standpoints. The federal government itself has various qualifying criteria for its different programs. The states have others. The CSS and ACT have another, which the college may or may not accept. At a conference I attended recently, a financial-aid officer complained that she frequently has to examine an application for aid from as many as four or five entirely different perspectives, each one purporting to be an evaluation of need. When colleges with large aid programs of their own are putting their own money on the line, they usually perform a careful, thoughtful analysis. The higher the percentage of government money, the less thorough the analysis.

THE INDEPENDENT STUDENT

This controversial category represents enormous potential savings for a family if it is willing to cut a child
off from all financial support and cast him out into the
world to fend for himself. He would no longer be able
to live with them, could visit no longer than six weeks
a year, and could legally receive very little assistance.

Once this maneuver is completed and the student
qualifies as an independent student, it's as though his
parents no longer exist. He can apply for financial aid
based on his income (which, if he went to college full-
time, would be zero except for what he could earn
during the summer and part-time during the school
year) and his assets (which in most cases would also
be zero). Needless to say, he would qualify for aid.
Moreover, his budget would require a twelve-month
analysis, since he wouldn't have any home to return to
during his vacation.

This category developed to process a type of student
who couldn't be processed any other way. This student was usually older than the average graduating
high-school senior, and frequently he was married
and even had children of his own. Such a student had
been out in the world and away from his parents for
some time, and the family relationship was such that
his parents no longer felt obligated to help with his
personal expenses. Financial-aid people reasoned that
students such as this were in fact independent of their
parents, and therefore they felt compelled to use the
student's income and assets to determine his eligibility for aid.

This, of course, created another problem. How
could financial-aid people assist the legitimate inde-

pendent student without enticing some parents to evade their financial responsibilities and let the public educate their children? The solution had to present difficulties sufficient to discourage bogus independent students without affecting the real ones. Time seemed the most useful criterion. To qualify as an independent student, a student:

1. Must not have lived or will not live with his parents for more than six weeks (forty-two days) during the calendar years just prior to or concurrent with college.
2. Must not have been or will not be listed as an exemption on his parents' income-tax return for the same calendar years.
3. Must not have received or will not receive assistance worth $750 or more from his parents during the same calendar years.

Let's see how this would work. A student who graduated from high school in June 1983 would have to wait until 1985 before he could qualify, since 1983 would not count as one of the two years he was on his own. Assuming he was self-supporting and out of the house in 1984, in 1985 he could qualify as an independent student. Since most aid has to be applied for in advance, it's doubtful whether he could receive sufficient for the spring semester of 1985, so he might have to mark time for two full years before he could begin college at the public's expense.

Students interested in this option might consider the armed forces as one useful way of passing time. Some college credits could be obtained while the prospective student was on active duty, and the Veterans' Educational Assistance Program (VEAP) could be an additional source of funds for college. Another plan might be for a student to attend college in the fall after he graduated from high school, since that year wouldn't count anyway as one of the magic two. After the fall semester he could drop out of college, get a job and an apartment, and wait until he qualified as an independent student.

There are some serious disadvantages to the independent student option. First, there is a moral question. Many people feel that it is highly unethical for families who can afford to pay for their children's educations to shirk this responsibility and let the public pick up the tab. Some financial-aid officers in particular feel strongly on this point and may not be as helpful as they would ordinarily be, if they suspect that a family is trying to pull a fast one.

Second, a waiting period is difficult for some students, especially if they are eager to begin life. The typical student graduates from college at twenty-two, but an independent student would be twenty-four or older. Moreover, some students will feel decidedly unhappy about seeing their friends going away to college while their parents not only tell them they can't go but kick them out of the door as well.

Third, it could be awkward socially. Parents love to boast that their child received a scholarship to Hogwash U., even though chances are that the scholarship was based purely on need (a point they neglect to mention); but it's a different thing to tell friends and relatives that Junior won't attend Hogwash U. this year after all but instead has an apartment of his own and some menial job. Parents who explain why will probably lose a few more social points.

Lastly, a few colleges have begun to tighten up by establishing more criteria than the government. Generally they have adopted twenty-six as the minimum age at which a student can be considered independent. One financial-aid officer with whom I chatted suspects that the federal government might move in this direction also, which would make financial aid more difficult. Another, however, doubts that this will happen.

The relative attractiveness of this option will probably vary over time, because there really is no good solution to the independent student concept. Whenever the criteria are lax, dependent students are tempted to become independent; and whenever they're stringent, valid independent students will have difficulty financing college. If the federal government were to tighten up, examples of unfortunate independent students would inevitably begin to surface, and before long the criteria would be loosened up again. This kind of maneuvering in the field of financial aid is constant.

I know of one person who attended college as an independent student and graduated twenty years ago. As he recalls, it was pretty tough financially the first year but after that it wasn't bad. And it saved his parents considerable expense. As long as financial need remains the basis for student aid, the category of independent student will continue to exist, although its appeal may wax and wane occasionally.

One word of advice. If you go this route, don't be halfhearted. Your child must have his own checking account and cancelled checks to prove that he pays rent. He must file his own income-tax return and not be listed on yours. Make the break a clean one. It would be ridiculous to have him leave home and mark time, and then be rejected for aid anyway.

CHEATING

One of the perennial problems associated with financial aid is that some families are dishonest. For instance, when New York state checked less than half of its applications for TAP (New York state aid) a couple of years ago, it was discovered that more than 23,500 students or families had cheated the state out of more than $5.3 million by understating their income. These fraudulent applications represented about 14 percent of the total. On the federal level, about 24 percent of the students receiving Pell Grants in 1980–81 supplied inaccurate information concerning their parents' incomes according to a study conducted for the United States Department of Education. Because of this and other errors made by students or aid officials, $100 million was overspent on just this single federal program of student aid in one year.

Morality aside, is cheating an attractive option? Let's analyze the situation, starting with the federal government. Beginning with the 1982–83 school year, an applicant for federal aid will receive a Student Aid Report (SAR), which he will have to take to his college. This SAR informs the college of the student's eligibility for federal aid through a Student Aid Index (SAI) number. If the SAR comes through starred, the information that has been supplied by the family must be validated by the college. Normally, in order to validate its application a family must mail to the college a verified or corrected SAR, a completed Validation Form, a signed copy of their 1040 tax return, and any other documents requested on the SAR.

In the past the federal government required validation for only about 10 percent of its applications and original plans were to increase this to 30 percent for 1982–83. But when the alarming results of the Pell Grant study became known, the government immediately increased the validation requirement to 100 percent. There's one difference, however. Since a complete validation by a college is a lengthy procedure, usually requiring much paperwork and correspondence between the college and the family, the government limited the current validation process to corrected SARs and copies of the 1040 tax return. One university with a high percentage of pupils receiving aid estimated that they would have had to double the size of their financial-aid staff in order to validate fully all SARs.

In the past most states checked a low percentage of their applications, but this, too, is changing. Many states, Pennsylvania, New York, New Jersey, and California, among them, are now checking most of the applications that come in. Moreover, unlike the federal government, which doesn't verify income information through the Internal Revenue Service, most states are checking applications directly against state income-tax returns. An applicant for aid in one of these states signs a waiver granting the state access to his tax return. Ideally, an applicant for federal aid should also be forced to sign such a waiver; financial-aid officers would welcome such a change.

The college aid office may pose the biggest hurdle of all. First, the college examines an applicant's finances and decides what he should receive from the federal and state governments. If the award that arrives is lower than anticipated, that's a signal to the college that the applicant may have given them a more creative account of his finances than he gave to the government. A cheater must tell the same lies to all three sources of aid. Second, colleges frequently receive unsolicited information from third parties. Sometimes students not on aid notice that a student receiving aid is better off than they are, or families brag to their friends about how they're cheating. One way or another much information wends its way to the financial-aid office. Third, a college can require a parent to sign a waiver granting it the right to verify his income-tax return directly with the Internal Revenue Service. This doesn't happen too often, but it is a possibility, especially with the current concern over cheating.

Families that cheat will have to avoid each of these three hazards for four years per child. Since applications are necessary for each student, a family with two in college has six rather than three chances to get caught each year. Perhaps some of the new validation checks won't be as thorough as they should be, but stringent or not, they're certainly worse than not being checked at all. Each year it will become harder to cheat successfully since more computers are being installed and more figures are being verified. Anyone caught providing false information to obtain federal student aid funds is subject to fines and/or imprisonment. State and local penalties may also apply.

Not only is cheating to obtain college aid wrong both legally and morally, but the sources of aid aren't quite the sitting ducks they once were. Thousands may have gotten away with it in the past, and no doubt thousands more will in the future, in spite of the increased surveillance. Even so, I'd recommend that my readers remain within the law. You'll sleep better!

5

ACCUMULATING ASSETS AND SHIFTING INCOME TO MINORS

A friend of mine has worked for many years in the field of tax and estate planning. Recently he observed that he has never met anyone who accumulated a large amount of money strictly from his salary. No matter how high someone's earnings, between the graduated income tax and the more expensive life-style to which he feels entitled as his income rises, his salary is largely dissipated. Anyone who does possess substantial assets has invariably obtained them through some other means: a successful business, stock options, an inheritance, or luck in investments.

Apparently, hard work alone may not be enough. There are so many leveling influences (the cost of a college education is itself one of these) that it is almost impossible for anyone to achieve his financial goals without serious investment and tax planning. The government takes too much in too many ways.

This section gathers together some of the tax and estate information and strategies most useful for families with children. While almost any family could benefit to some extent from this information, some of my suggestions are most suitable for those that possess the kind of earnings and/or assets that would make tax considerations important. Time is another factor. To receive maximum benefits, families should begin using some of these strategies when their children are still young, not wait until they're within a year or so of college. A final consideration is the possibility of college financial aid. As was explained previously, families that hope for aid should avoid giving assets to their children.

Although the most popular strategies will be covered, readers should recognize that their specific situations might suggest to a skilled adviser other plans not even mentioned. This is merely a survey to acquaint the reader with the types of options that exist—a place to start, not stop.

THE UNIFORM GIFTS TO MINORS ACT

Probably the easiest way to accumulate capital for a college education is to place assets in a child's name under the Uniform Gifts to Minors Act. When parents retain these assets, all of the income generated is taxed at their highest tax bracket; but a child pays no taxes until he receives $1,000 of unearned income a year (versus $2,300 of earned income). Even if the child has to pay taxes, they're relatively low; and the parents can continue to claim him as a deduction. The lowest tax bracket is 12 percent in 1982 and 11 percent in 1983 and later years, a far cry from the average parent's bracket.

Setting up this plan is simplicity itself. A parent merely lists the stocks, bonds, certificates, or other assets in the names of the child and a custodian. The account might read: John B. Jones, Custodian for John B. Jones, Jr., under the Uniform Gifts to Minors Act. When earnings are generated by the investment, they are reported to the government with the child's, rather than the parent's, Social Security number.

In spite of the tax advantage of this situation, parents should realize that they have made a permanent gift of these assets. They cannot regain them for their personal use or use them to pay for items for the child that are considered part of their support obligation. In short, they can't use the money to buy him clothes or a stereo. That money can pay for his college education, however, since a parent isn't obligated to finance a college education for his child unless he has agreed to do so, typically as part of a divorce settlement.

A problem arises if the donor also becomes the custodian, since the IRS could claim that the donor retained effective control over the assets. For instance, let's say a grandmother gave stock to her grandchild, named herself custodian, and later died. That stock would become part of her estate.

Since parents, too, could face this problem, some planning is in order. If the husband is the sole wage-earner, the wife should be the custodian. If both parents work, records should be kept to prove that a differentiation exists. If the mother is the donor, she should write the check donating the money, and the father should be the custodian.

As a practical matter, the IRS isn't closely monitoring the Uniform Gifts to Minors Act. The vast majority of families that establish such gifts will never hear one word from the government. Nevertheless, people should recognize the technicalities.

THE 2503-C TRUST

This close relative of the Uniform Gifts to Minors Act is useful whenever a substantial gift is contemplated, perhaps by a grandparent. This trust has two advantages: First, it can be more flexible, since the provisions are established by the trust when it is drawn rather than by a state law; second, it can continue past the beneficiary's twenty-first birthday if the trust is written with this in mind. The chief disadvantage would be the cost of establishing the trust, since a lawyer would be necessary.

ESTATE PLANNING

Gift-giving could also prove useful insofar as estate planning is concerned. Although the Economic Recovery Act of 1981 freed most families from the worry of federal estate taxes, there are still some, again typically grandparents, who might consider their effect.

Donors are now able to give $10,000 per year free of any gift taxes ($20,000 per year if spouses are both giving). Moreover, certain expenses such as tuition or medical bills are excluded. Therefore, a grandparent could give a gift of $10,000 per year to a grandchild and, in addition, pay his college tuition (directly to the college, not through the parents) without incurring a gift tax. If an estate is above the lifetime free-gift limit, spreading a few of those ten thousands around per recipient per year could save tremendously on estate taxes.

Luckily, the new law raised the level at which federal estate taxes begin, which is why most families should escape. Here are the new minimums:

1982	$225,000	1985	$400,000
1983	$275,000	1986	$500,000
1984	$325,000	1987 and after	$600,000

Although these totals look impressive, keep in mind that we're not up to $600,000 yet, and many families could still be affected. We now have an average family net worth of $104,000 in this country, largely because so many families own homes that have increased in value. If $104,000 is average, estate taxes are far from extinct.

The new law also eliminated the concept of "anticipation of death." Under this old rule, a gift was normally included in the estate if the donor died within three years of making the gift. Consequently, there could now be some deathbed sharing of the wealth at $10,000 per person. More than $10,000 per person per year isn't as worthwhile, since the excess would have to be included in the estate for tax purposes, in any case.

This brief discussion of the value of gifts in estate planning is oriented toward families with children. As an estate-tax strategy, however, gift-giving is merely one of many options, and families who face inheritance taxes should consider a more comprehensive examination of their problem. Well-planned trusts, for instance, can significantly reduce estate taxes without jeopardizing an older couple's economic well-being or hampering their life-style. Banks, insurance companies, brokerage firms, and lawyers who specialize in estate planning can all offer further information and services. Frequently they can also help with other tax strategies, such as deferring or decreasing income taxes, which are also mentioned earlier.

TAX-SHELTERED ANNUITIES

I have already discussed tax-sheltered annuities that reduce a worker's earned income. Well, here's a different type.

Let's say parents have money set aside and earmarked for a child's education. If they invest these funds in traditional ways, income taxes will inhibit their growth. Placed in a tax-sheltered annuity, on the other hand, these funds could blossom in a tax-free environment. Moreover, when the child reached college age, the parents could withdraw their original principal free of any tax and use it for tuition. The remainder, which over the years would have grown to a sizable sum, could be left intact until the parents' retirement, when their tax rates would decrease. One of the beauties of this strategy is that the assets always belong to the parents.

It now appears that Congress or the IRS might decide to make this a less attractive option. Critics claim that this annuity, unlike other tax-sheltered annuities which limit contributions and in which *all* of the money is tax-sheltered, is more a tax-avoidance scheme than a bona-fide annuity. Therefore, it would be wise to investigate the legal status of this investment when you wish to use it (a wise idea with any investment). Perhaps this annuity will last fifty years—or maybe only fifty days.

THE CLIFFORD TRUST

Many families would love to shift income from themselves to their child by means of the Uniform Gifts to

Minors Act, but they're reluctant to give up the principal. The Clifford Trust is one means of accomplishing this.

To establish a Clifford Trust, a parent must place income-producing assets in a trust, naming the child as beneficiary and a third party (neither parent) as trustee. This trust must last for at least ten years and a day; the assets then revert to the parent.

The chief advantages of this plan are that it shifts income to the minor, that the parents regain the principal, and that this principal can consist of securities, real estate, or cash.

The chief disadvantages are that it must last so long that any income generated by the trust cannot be used for the child's support, that any capital gains taken by the trust are taxable to the parent (since the parent actually owns them), that the income from the trust is considered a gift from the donor to the beneficiary (which could have significance if the estate is sufficiently large to pay estate taxes), and that it's generally not economically worthwhile to establish this trust for amounts of less than $10,000.

In spite of its drawbacks, this plan could prove attractive to some families. A lawyer would be required to analyze the trust in detail and do the paperwork.

THE CROWN LOAN

Many people feel that this plan has all of the advantages of the Clifford Trust and almost none of the disadvantages. Unfortunately, while the courts have on several occasions held that the Crown Loan is absolutely legal, the IRS doesn't agree. Let's examine it anyway, since it's so very attractive. Here's how it works:

A parent loans money (it's better to avoid securities) to a child at no interest (this avoids the gift tax) and with no maturity date. The loan is simply repayable in full to the parent on demand. Thus, the parent transfers income to the child but retains his right to the principal whenever he wants it, not after ten years, as in a Clifford Trust.

To structure this properly, a trust must be established if the beneficiary is an unemancipated minor (in most states someone under eighteen), since a minor cannot borrow. After the loan is advanced, there should occasionally be some repayment, since it could otherwise be called an invalid debt. Finally, the loan should be called in after about five years and a new one established, because loans that aren't demanded within a certain time (usually six years) become invalid. Normally, no money is distributed to the child if the trust is in effect (unlike the Clifford Trust, which does distribute income), and taxes are paid by the trust.

The advantages of this loan are that it transfers income from a high tax bracket to a low one, that it allows the parent to regain his capital at any time, and that the income can be used for support of the child.

The only major disadvantage is that the IRS could decide to contest the case if they discover the loan. Most observers don't worry about this because they feel, first, that the IRS will uncover relatively few of these loans and, second, that nothing illegal is being done anyway since the courts have found it to be legal. If you happen to be one of those that they do chance upon, though, you would probably have to decide whether to fight it in court with precedent on your side or give up and pay what you're assessed.

For those willing to accept the risk of IRS disapproval, the Crown Loan is a terrific idea. As with the

Clifford Trust, a lawyer should set it up, and the loan should be large enough to make a trust economical.

For those in a high tax bracket, 50 percent, for instance, an intriguing option involving the Crown Loan is to borrow the money and lend it to the child. The math works this way. Typically there's a spread of about 3 to 4 percent between the cost of borrowing and the earnings from investing. Thus, if a parent borrowed at 16 percent (which becomes 8 percent for someone in the 50 percent bracket) and the child earned 12 percent, with few taxes in an investment such as a bank certificate or money market, a family could benefit from a Crown Loan even if it had no spare cash of its own to lend.

II
Need-Based Financial Aid

6

THE PROGRAMS

FEDERAL PROGRAMS

PELL GRANT

The Pell Grant, which until 1981–82 was known as the Basic Educational Opportunity Grant, is the only federal grant that must be applied for directly. Currently Pell Grants range from $200 to $1,674 per academic year, although there is statutory authority for them to reach $1,800. In order to be eligible for a Pell Grant (and usually most other federal aid), an applicant must be enrolled at least half-time (usually defined as six credit hours per term) in an eligible program at a college, university, vocational school, technical school, or hospital school of nursing that participates in federal financial-aid programs. Undergraduates are eligible for both the Pell Grants and the other federal programs that will be described, but graduate students are ineligible for Pell Grants and Supplemental Educational Opportunity Grants.

As with all federal programs, a student must make satisfactory progress in order to remain eligible for aid. For instance, if a full-time student earns only twenty credits during his first year in college, he is ineligible for aid during his second year since he's still a freshman. Also, federal aid is good for only eight semesters or twelve terms. Therefore, if a student changes majors and takes five years to graduate, he is ineligible for aid his last year. Students majoring in architecture, which is normally a five-year program, are ineligible their fifth year. Students involved in cooperative education generally qualify for aid for all five years since they're in school only eight semesters or twelve terms spread over five years.

The Pell Grant, like Social Security, is an entitlement program. Therefore a recipient of this grant is entitled to it as a matter of right, and expenditures for this program will fluctuate depending upon the number of eligible applicants. Other federal programs are campus based, and awards are distributed as set amounts per institution. An eligible applicant may be denied campus-based aid if the institution receives insufficient aid to accommodate all who qualify.

CAMPUS-BASED PROGRAMS

Unlike the Pell Grant, which is awarded to a recipient directly by the government, the following three federal programs are campus based. No special application is necessary. College financial-aid officers automatically award them to eligible applicants for aid. These officers are expected to offer these awards to the neediest of their students, and the government can eliminate an institution from the program if it deviates from this policy.

Nevertheless, provided they remain within federal parameters, institutions can use their own rather than federal criteria for establishing need for campus-based aid. This is a crucial difference, since many colleges feel that their need analysis is more sophisticated than the federal one and that the Pell Grant

Program sometimes over- or under-awards aid to applicants. Differences between federal and college need analyses are most pronounced at colleges that use the FAF, since the government does not use Side II of this form and most of these questions are missing from the FFS. Factors that some colleges and the government treat differently include:

1. Home equity: Colleges consider the year of purchase and purchase price in their analysis, but the government doesn't.
2. Other household members in college: Colleges analyze how many other members in the home attend college and the costs of the colleges that they attend. These are not considered by the government.
3. Divorce and separation: Colleges want information concerning the absent, natural parent. Federal analysis omits this parent.
4. Business expenses and tax losses: Colleges feel that a losing investment should not be allowed to shelter income from other sources. Government analysis permits tax losses.
5. Special circumstances: Colleges are more ready to deal subjectively with unusual family situations. Strictly following the rules, the government wants the numbers.

The following are the three campus-based programs:

Supplemental Educational Opportunity Grant (SEOG). These grants range from $200 to $2,000 in value per academic year. Of the three campus-based programs, SEOG is by far the most desirable since it is an outright grant and need not be repaid. Since a school may elect to use up to 10 percent of its SEOG money for less than half-time students, it may be possible for such a student to qualify for an SEOG.

National Direct Student Loans (NDSL). An NDSL is the most favorable loan that a borrower can obtain. Eligible students may borrow up to $3,000 if enrolled in a vocational school for the first two years of college and up to $6,000 for the full four years of undergraduate study. Graduate students may borrow up to $12,000, but this maximum includes whatever they may have borrowed as undergraduates. The interest rate of 5 percent and repayment both begin six months after graduation or leaving school. No payments are required for up to three years while the student serves in the armed forces, Peace Corps, Vista, or the Commissioned Corps of the Public Health Service. There are also possible loan cancellations for borrowers who enter certain fields of teaching or specified military occupations.

The College Work-Study Program (CWSP). The CWSP provides jobs for eligible students by subsidizing the wages they receive. Since all employment must be confined to nonprofit institutions, most college students are hired for on-campus jobs. Vocational schools experience greater difficulty locating permissible jobs since most of them are profitmaking. Students in these jobs cannot work beyond the amount for which they are budgeted. For instance, a student who is awarded $1,000 in CWS cannot continue working after he has earned the $1,000, unless his employer begins funding the job. As with an SEOG, it may be possible for a less than half-time student to qualify for CWS.

Institutions are awarded campus-based aid under a complicated formula, and once a school exhausts its aid for the year, it cannot make further awards. Some of the ramifications of the funding formula are:

First of all, since campus-based aid is first awarded by state and then by institution within each state, the size of an institution's campus-based program is partially attributable to its location. Consequently, institutions located in states with relatively small numbers of low-income residents are more likely to have sufficient campus-based aid than institutions located in states with large numbers of such residents.

Secondly, institutions with high percentages of commuting and/or part-time students generally receive more ample supplies of campus-based aid. Typically, these are public institutions with tuitions already low in comparison to private schools. A student at a public institution sometimes discovers that he has no need for a loan or job since the cost of his education is modest and his grants and parental aid are sufficient to meet his expenses. His counterpart at a private institution, on the other hand, generally finds that he needs a grant, a loan, and a job in addition to assistance from home. Undergraduates who finish college heavily in debt have almost invariably attended private institutions.

FEDERAL AID STATISTICS

The following tables provide excellent insight into the dimensions and dynamics of federal aid programs. Tables 5.5 and 6.2 were taken from a United States Department of Education research document entitled *Study of Program Management Procedures in the Campus-Based and Basic Grant Program,* by Robert T. Deane, et al., June, 1980. Although the data relate to the 1978–79 school year, these programs have not changed significantly since that time despite inflation. If anything, the statistics may paint too rosy a picture.

Table 5.5 illustrates the distribution of federal student-aid awards by income level and dependency status. Note that the Basic Educational Opportunity Grant Program has been renamed the Pell Grant Program. This table shows that Pell Grants are for the most part confined to the lowest three income categories, while the three campus-based programs reach a wider range of families. This difference arises because the officials in charge of campus-based programs try to take more into account than income. Even though certain families may have higher incomes than Pell Grant families, their educational expenses may be far greater, too.

Table 6.2 illustrates the percentage of aid applicants by income level and dependency status whose financial need is satisfied by grants rather than jobs. Most observers feel that students who receive grants should be required to assume part of the burden themselves through jobs and loans. This table shows that sizable percentages of financial aid applicants at proprietary schools and four- and two-year public colleges and universities hold no loan or work burden and receive, in effect, a "free ride," as the author of the study termed it. Students at private colleges and universities are not as lucky, especially if they are dependent. Unless it's in the position to offer aid of its own, a private college can prove to have been an expensive choice for a student, even when he is able to qualify for financial aid.

THE GUARANTEED STUDENT LOAN (GSL)

In addition to the previously described aid, the federal government sponsors two additional loan programs: the Guaranteed Student Loan (GSL) and the

Parent Loan. Superficially, these programs may appear to be state programs, but the federal government originated the concepts and supplied the backing. States merely operate the programs.

The maximum GSL is $2,500 and the interest rate is 9 percent for full-time undergraduates. Half-time undergraduates may borrow up to $1,250 a year. Full-time graduates may borrow up to $5,000 each year and half-time $2,500. The loan is interest free while the student is in school, and interest begins six months after the borrower graduates or leaves school. A "loan origination fee" of 5 percent is charged for these loans; so if your need is defined as $2,000, you will actually receive only $1,900. If you talk to your college financial aid officer, he can certify a higher need so that you actually receive the $2,000 that you theoretically need.

Prior to 1981–82 these loans were available to any student, regardless of income. Since then, families with less than $30,000 a year income have been eligible, and many families with higher incomes have also been eligible provided they could prove financial need. While the need test for the over-$30,000 incomes has been surprisingly flexible, it appears that it may become more stringent. Moreover, the government may begin other economy measures because GSL become a very expensive aid program.

Generally, these loans are easily available through banks. If you do have a problem finding one, ask a nearby college which local banks carry them. Since these loans are made to the student and guaranteed by the state, the state is responsible for any defaulted loan. If the student is under eighteen, however, a parent must cosign for this loan, and that parent will be held responsible if the student defaults.

TABLE 5.5: ESTIMATED PERCENTAGE DISTRIBUTION OF FEDERAL STUDENT FINANCIAL ASSISTANCE PROGRAMS FOR UNDERGRADUATE STUDENTS BY FAMILY INCOME AND DEPENDENCY STATUS: ACADEMIC YEAR 1978–79

	Total Recipients (Percentage)	Total Awards (Percentage)	Average Award (Dollars)	PERCENTAGE ALL STUDENTS
A. BASIC EDUCATIONAL OPPORTUNITY GRANT PROGRAM				
ALL STUDENTS	100.0%	100.0%		
Dependents				
$0–$5,999	20.2	23.6	1089	5.5
$6,000–$11,999	24.6	26.2	996	8.4
$12,000–$17,999	14.1	10.7	702	11.7
$18,000–$24,999	3.7	2.1	532	13.5
$25,000–$29,999	0.4	0.3	704	6.0
$30,000 or more	0.1	0.1	739	16.4
Independents	31.3	31.2	927	38.4
Unknown*	5.6	5.7		
B. SUPPLEMENTAL EDUCATIONAL OPPORTUNITY GRANT PROGRAM				
ALL STUDENTS	100.0%	100.0%		
Dependents				
$0–$5,999	16.9	15.9	596	5.5
$6,000–$11,999	20.5	19.1	592	8.4
$12,000–$17,999	17.6	17.5	628	11.7
$18,000–$24,999	9.6	9.8	650	13.5
$25,000–$29,999	1.9	1.9	635	6.0
$30,000 or more	0.7	0.6	560	16.4
Independents	29.9	32.7	693	38.4
Unknown*	2.9	2.5		

*Students of unknown dependency status and/or income level.
SOURCE: Student financial aid records.

TABLE 5.5: ESTIMATED PERCENTAGE DISTRIBUTION OF FEDERAL STUDENT FINANCIAL ASSISTANCE PROGRAMS FOR UNDERGRADUATE STUDENTS BY FAMILY INCOME AND DEPENDENCY STATUS: ACADEMIC YEAR 1978–79 (continued)

	Total Recipients (Percentage)	Total Awards (Percentage)	Average Award (Dollars)	PERCENTAGE ALL STUDENTS
C. NATIONAL DIRECT STUDENT LOAN PROGRAM				
ALL STUDENTS	100.0%	100.0%		
Dependents				
$0–$5,999	10.4	9.3	722	5.5
$6,000–$11,999	16.5	14.4	704	8.4
$12,000–$17,999	18.9	16.9	724	11.7
$18,000–$24,999	15.9	16.9	834	13.5
$25,000–$29,999	3.9	4.1	820	6.0
$30,000 or more	2.0	2.0	746	16.4
Independents	26.4	30.2	951	38.4
Unknown*	6.0	6.7		
D. COLLEGE WORK-STUDY PROGRAM				
ALL STUDENTS	100.0%	100.0%		
Dependents				
$0–$5,999	16.3	16.3	848	5.5
$6,000–$11,999	18.0	17.5	822	8.4
$12,000–$17,999	16.9	15.6	780	11.7
$18,000–$24,999	13.2	12.3	791	13.5
$25,000–$29,999	3.8	2.9	652	6.0
$30,000 or more	1.9	1.6	696	16.4
Independents	22.7	27.3	1018	38.4
Unknown*	7.2	6.5		

*Students of unknown dependency status and/or income level.
SOURCE: Student financial aid records.

Formerly, some students were declaring bank-ruptcy and defaulting on loans, but this has become more difficult. Student loans can no longer be can-celled through bankruptcy until five years after a student leaves college. During those five years if a student is in arrears, he is listed as a poor credit risk and will be unable to borrow money for a car or a home. Garnishment of wages is also a possibility.

Neither the GSL nor the Parent Loan, which will be described next, can exceed the cost of education:

> $7,000 cost of education
> − $5,000 aid received (Pell, SEOG,
> _____ CWSP, college, etc.)
> $2,000 maximum that can be borrowed.

THE PARENT LOAN

The Parent Loan sometimes is referred to as PLUS (Parent Loan for Undergraduate Students) and some-times as ALAS (Auxiliary Loans to Assist Students). The problem is that the program began as PLUS, but then it was decided that this was misleading since the borrower could be a student instead of a parent. Consequently, the acronym was changed to ALAS, which merely confused everyone. Some financial aid material even describes PLUS and ALAS as two sepa-rate programs. Since it's still new, the Parent Loan is not yet available in all states.

The Parent Loan is available to any parent of a dependent college student regardless of financial need, provided the loan doesn't exceed the cost of

TABLE 6.2: PERCENTAGE OF UNDERGRADUATE AID APPLICANTS WITH LOAN-WORK BURDENS OF ZERO PERCENT, BY INSTITUTION LEVEL AND CONTROL AND TOTAL FAMILY INCOME: ACADEMIC YEAR 1978–79

| | ALL APPLICANTS | Institutional Level and Control | | | | |
		4-Year Public	4-Year Private	2-Year Public	2-Year Private	Propri-etary
Dependents						
$0–$5,999	33	44	9	31	9	37
$6,000–$11,999	28	34	9	37	5	34
$12,000–$17,999	12	13	2	25	3	30
$18,000–$24,999	5	5	3	21	0	4
$25,000–$29,999	4	7	0	30	3	*
$30,000 or more	2	8	0	*	*	0
Independents						
$0–$2,999	30	23	12	48	21	24
$3,000–$5,999	39	28	18	58	14	29
$6,000–$8,999	43	41	34	43	22	63
$9,000–$11,999	33	39	5	36	*	*
$12,000–$14,999	23	22	*	*	*	*
$15,000 or more	13	8	14	*	*	*

*Students of unknown dependency status and/or income level.
SOURCE: Student financial aid records.

education minus financial aid. The interest rate is 14 percent, and the payments begin sixty days after the commencement of the loan. If interest rates fall, the government will lower the 14 percent interest of the Parent Loan to keep it slightly more favorable than normal commercial loans. Parents may borrow as much as $3,000 per year and up to $15,000 maximum for each child.

A graduate student enrolled at least half time may borrow as much as $3,000 per year and up to $15,000 maximum. In addition, a graduate student may also take out a GSL as long as the total of the two loans doesn't exceed the cost of education minus financial aid.

An independent undergraduate enrolled at least half time may borrow up to $2,500 provided this doesn't exceed the cost of education minus financial aid. If the student has also obtained a GSL, the total of the two loans cannot exceed $2,500. The maximum that an independent undergraduate may borrow under both the Parent Loan and the GSL is $12,500.

OTHER FEDERAL PROGRAMS

Most other federal aid programs that were intended for specific students, those pursuing certain majors, for instance, either have been discontinued or are in the process of being phased out (open only to those who previously qualified). There are two remaining: one for students of Indian descent and the other for graduate students in the health fields.

American Indian Grants and Loans. Needy students who have at least one-fourth Indian blood and who are members of an Indian tribe are eligible for both grants and loans. Information and applications are available through the home agency, tribe, or area office. Further information may be obtained from the Bureau Scholarship Officer, Office of Indian Education Programs, Bureau of Indian Affairs, 18th and C Streets, N.W., Washington, D.C., 20245.

Health Education Assistance Loan (HEAL) Program. Graduate students in medicine, osteopathy, dentistry, veterinary medicine, optometry, podiatry, public health, pharmacy, chiropractics, or in programs in health administration or clinical psychology are eligible for federally insured loans under the HEAL Program. This loan does not provide a subsidy for interest, but it does make large amounts of money, as much as $20,000 per student per year, available for these students. Further information and applications are available through the health professions schools.

STATE PROGRAMS

The financial efforts that states make in their assistance programs differ widely. Five states—New York, Pennsylvania, Illinois, California, and New Jersey—provide more assistance than all of the rest of the states put together. Some of the discrepancies in efforts are obvious in the following list. What isn't as obvious is that many states don't come close to fulfilling in fact what they offer in theory. For instance, one state was candid enough to disclose that it helped only 34 percent of its *eligible* applicants for aid in 1981–82 because the legislature didn't appropriate sufficient funds. This is a common problem, and most state awards are relatively modest in comparison to federal.

One unfortunate aspect of state programs is that most states don't permit their aid to leave the state. If such a state has a substantial aid program of its own (New York and California are examples), a needy student is pressured to remain in state. Private colleges located close to New York or California sometimes make especially favorable financial-aid offers to students from these states in order to maintain matriculation patterns with these students. Even so, it's a difficult situation, and some students would be wise to apply in state at least as a backup if their first choice is out of state.

The state programs listed are those of general interest. Many states also offer grants or loans that are available to unusual students: dependents of policemen who died while on duty, dependents of a member of the armed forces who was killed during wartime, or students of American Indian heritage. High school guidance offices should have leaflets describing all of the programs offered by their states. Otherwise, write to the address listed.

ALABAMA

Alabama Student Assistance Program. Awards grants worth $300 to residents for undergraduate study at in-state institutions.

Alabama Student Grant Program. Awards grants to residents for undergraduate study at certain in-state private colleges and universities. Applications are available through eligible institutions.

Alabama Nursing Scholarship Program. Awards

scholarships/grants to residents enrolled in in-state nursing programs. Applications are available through the programs.

For further information, write Alabama Commission on Higher Education, Student Assistance, Suite 221, One Court Square, Montgomery, Alabama 36197.

ALASKA

Alaska Student Loan Program. Provides loans of up to $6,000 undergraduate and $7,000 graduate per year at 5 percent interest. Student must have been an Alaska resident for at least two years and must be a full-time student at an approved vocational school or an accredited college or university. Recipients who reside in Alaska after completion of studies may be eligible for a cancellation of up to 50 percent of the loan.

Alaska State Educational Incentive Grant Program. Awards grants worth from $100 to $1,500 to residents for study at undergraduate colleges or universities.

WICHE Student Exchange Program. Allows residents who wish to major in any of sixteen fields not available in Alaska to study in other states at reduced tuitions.

For further information, write Alaska Commission on Postsecondary Education, Pouch FP, Juneau, Alaska 99811.

ARIZONA

Arizona State Student Incentive Grant Program. Awards grants worth up to $2,000 to residents for full-time undergraduate study at in-state institutions.

For further information, write Arizona Commission for Postsecondary Education, 1650 Alameda Drive, Suite 115, Tempe, Arizona 85028.

ARKANSAS

Arkansas State Scholarship Program. Awards grants worth from $100 to $300 based on both financial need and academic criteria to residents for full-time undergraduate study at in-state institutions.

For further information, write Arkansas Department of Higher Education, 1301 West Seventh Street, Little Rock, Arkansas 72201.

CALIFORNIA

Cal Grant A. Assists with the tuitions of low- and middle-income residents at in-state colleges and universities. Grants range from $600 to $3,400 at independent colleges, $300 to full fees at the University of California, and average $250 at the California State University and Colleges.

Cal Grant B. Provides a living allowance and tuition help for very low-income residents who attend in-state colleges and universities. The living allowance grant ranges from $500 to $1,100, and the tuition award grant ranges from $250 at state colleges to $3,200 at private colleges.

Cal Grant C. Assists residents attending in-state vocational and technical schools. Grants range up to $2,000 for tuition and $500 for training related costs.

For further information, write California Student Aid Commission, 1410 Fifth Street, Sacramento, California 95814.

COLORADO

Colorado Student Grant Program. Awards grants worth up to $1,000 to residents for undergraduate study at in-state public institutions.

Scholarship Program for Undergraduate Students. Awards scholarships worth $500 to residents for undergraduate study at in-state public institutions.

For further information, write Colorado Commission on Higher Education, 1550 Lincoln Street, Denver, Colorado 80203.

CONNECTICUT

Scholastic Achievement Grant Program. Awards grants worth from $1,000 to $1,500 at private in-state institutions; from $100 to $500 at in-state public institutions; and up to $500 for out-of-state institutions located in District of Columbia, Maryland, Massachusetts, New Hampshire, Pennsylvania, Rhode Island, or Vermont. Eligible residents must be enrolled as full-time undergraduates. The grant is based on both financial need and academic criteria (top 10 percent of high school class or 1200 or better SAT score).

Connecticut Grant for Study at Independent Colleges. Awards grants to residents for full-time undergraduate study at in-state private institutions.

For further information, write Board of Higher Education, 61 Woodland Street, Hartford, Connecticut 06105.

DELAWARE

Postsecondary Scholarship Fund. Awards grants worth up to $700 to residents for full-time study at colleges or universities located in Delaware, Maryland, and Pennsylvania. Normally this grant is intended for undergraduate study, but graduate students are also eligible if the graduate program is not offered within Delaware.

For further information, write Postsecondary Education Commission, 820 French Street, Carvel State Office Building, Wilmington, Delaware 19801.

DISTRICT OF COLUMBIA

Student Incentive Grant Program. Awards grants worth up to $1,500 to residents for full-time undergraduate study at Washington, D.C., institutions.

For further information, write to the Washington, D.C., institution you wish to attend.

FLORIDA

Florida Student Assistance Grant. Awards grants worth up to $1,200 to two-year residents for full-time study at in-state institutions.

Florida Tuition Voucher. Awards grants worth up to $1,000 to two-year residents for full-time study at in-state private colleges or universities.

For further information, write Florida Student Financial Assistance Commission, Knott Building, Tallahassee, Florida 32301.

GEORGIA

Georgia Student Incentive Grant. Awards grants worth from $150 to $450 to residents for full-time undergraduate study at in-state institutions.

Georgia Private College Tuition Equalization Grant. Awards grants worth $650 to residents attending in-state private colleges or universities.

For further information, write Georgia Student Finance Authority, 9 La Vista Perimeter Park, Suite 110, Tucker, Georgia 30084.

HAWAII

Hawaii State Scholarships. Awards grants to residents for full-time study at the University of Hawaii.

Hawaii Tuition Waivers. Awards tuition waivers to residents or nonresidents for full-time study at the University of Hawaii.

Hawaii Student Incentive Grants. Awards grants to residents who qualify for a Pell Grant and who study full time at the University of Hawaii.

For further information, write to the branch of the University of Hawaii you wish to attend.

IDAHO

State of Idaho Scholarship Program. Awards scholarships worth $1,500 to graduating-senior residents for full-time undergraduate study at in-state colleges or universities. This scholarship is based both on the student's rank in class and his American College Testing scores.

State Student Incentive Grant Program. Awards grants worth up to $2,000 to residents for at least half-time undergraduate study at in-state institutions.

For further information, write Office of Higher Education, 650 West State Street, Boise, Idaho 83720.

ILLINOIS

Illinois Academic Scholarship Program. Awards scholarships worth $1,000 to two thousand residents on the basis of academic excellence rather than financial need for study at in-state colleges and universities.

Illinois Monetary Award Program. Awards grants worth up to $1,950 to residents for full-time undergraduate study at in-state colleges, universities, schools of nursing, or allied health programs. Students at vocational or technical schools are ineligible.

For further information, write Illinois State Scholarship Commission, Office of Informational Services, 525 West Jefferson Street, Springfield, Illinois 62702.

INDIANA

Indiana Hoosier Scholar Awards. Awards $500 non-renewable scholarships to residents based on academic excellence for study at in-state postsecondary institutions.

Indiana Higher Education Awards. Awards grants to residents for full-time study at in-state postsecondary institutions.

Indiana Freedom of Choice Grants. Awards grants to residents who received a maximum Higher Education Award and who plan to attend in-state private institutions.

For further information, write State Student Assistance Commission of Indiana, 219 North Senate Avenue, Indianapolis, Indiana 46202.

IOWA

Iowa Tuition Grant Program. Awards grants worth up to $1,700 to residents for study at in-state private colleges, business schools, and hospital schools of nursing.

Iowa Vocational-Technical Tuition Grant Program. Awards grants worth up to $400 to residents for study at in-state vocational or technical schools.

Iowa Scholarship Program. Awards grants worth up to $600 to residents based on both academic and financial criteria for study at in-state postsecondary institutions.

For further information, write Iowa College Aid Commission, 201 Jewett Building, Ninth and Grand, Des Moines, Iowa 50309.

KANSAS

Kansas State Scholarship Program. Awards grants worth up to $500 to residents based on the results of the American College Testing assessment or the Career Planning Profile plus financial need for study at in-state postsecondary institutions.

Kansas Tuition Grant Program. Awards grants worth up to $1,200 to residents for study at in-state private colleges or universities.

Higher Education Loan Program (HELP) of Kansas. Loans money directly to students unable to obtain loans through commercial lenders. Residents attending in-state or out-of-state and nonresidents attending Kansas postsecondary institutions are eligible.

For further information, write State of Kansas Board of Regents, Suite 1416, Merchants National Bank Tower, Topeka, Kansas 66612.

KENTUCKY

Kentucky Higher Education Assistance Authority (KHEAA) Grants. Awards grants ranging from $200 to $1,150 to residents for full-time nonreligious study at eligible in-state institutions.

For further information, write Kentucky Higher Education Assistance Authority, 1050 U.S. 127 South, Frankfort, Kentucky 40601.

LOUISIANA

Louisiana Academic, Centennial, or Decennial Scholarships. Awards scholarships to residents based on academic and other achievement, class rank, tests, interviews, and recommendations. Recipient must attend an in-state public institution.

State Student Incentive Grant. Awards grants worth from $200 to $1,500 to residents who have at least a 2.0 grade point average to attend in-state institutions.

T. H. Harris Scholarships. Awards scholarships worth $250 to residents with a *B* average in high school and participation in extracurricular activities.

Rockefeller Scholarships. Awards academic scholarships worth $1,000 per year to residents majoring in forestry, wildlife, fisheries, or marine science at an in-state state-supported institution.

For further information, write Governor's Special Commission on Education Services, P. O. Box 44127, Baton Rouge, Louisiana 70804.

MAINE

Maine Student Incentive Scholarship Program. Awards grants worth from $200 to $1,500 to residents for full-time undergraduate study in Maine and Massachusetts.

For further information, write State Department of Educational and Cultural Services, State House Station 23, Augusta, Maine 04333.

MARYLAND

Maryland General State Scholarship. Awards grants worth from $200 to $1,500 to residents for full-time undergraduate study. No more than 10 percent of the awards can be granted to students attending college out-of-state.

Senatorial Scholarships. Awards grants worth from $200 to $1,500 to residents for full-time undergraduate study in Maryland or at an out-of-state institution if the college major is not offered in Maryland. This grant is based on both academic credentials and financial need.

House of Delegate Scholarships. Awards scholarships worth up to the price of tuition and fees at the University of Maryland to residents for full-time undergraduate study. Since there are few of these awards, students should contact their delegates directly rather than the State Scholarship Board.

Distinguished Scholar Awards. Awards scholarships worth $800 to three hundred residents each year for full-time study within Maryland.

For further information, write Maryland State Scholarship Board, 2100 Guilford Avenue, Baltimore, Maryland 21218.

MASSACHUSETTS

Massachusetts General Scholarship Program. Awards grants worth from $300 to $900 to residents for full-time undergraduate study within Massachusetts, Connecticut, District of Columbia, Maine, Maryland, New Hampshire, New Jersey, Pennsylvania, Rhode Island, or Vermont.

Massachusetts Honor Scholarship Program. Awards scholarships worth the cost of tuition at an in-state, state-supported, four-year institution to residents who obtain one of the four highest SAT scores in their state senatorial districts.

For further information, write Board of Regents of Higher Education, Scholarship Office, 330 Stuart Street, Boston, Massachusetts 02116.

MICHIGAN

Michigan Competitive Scholarship Program. Awards grants worth up to $1,200 to residents based on both a qualifying score on an American College Test and financial need for full-time study at a Michigan institution.

Michigan Tuition Grant Program. Awards grants worth up to $1,300 to residents for study at private Michigan colleges and universities.

Legislative Merit Award Program. Awards a nonrenewable scholarship to residents based on the American College Test for study at any United States college or university.

Differential Grant Program. Awards a grant worth $500 to residents for full- or part-time study at an in-state private college or university. Financial need is not a factor in this award.

For further information, write Department of Education, P.O. Box 30008, Lansing, Michigan 48909.

MINNESOTA

Minnesota Scholarship Program. Awards grants worth from $100 to $1,400 to residents based on high school class rank and financial need for undergraduate study at in-state postsecondary institutions.

Minnesota Grant-in-Aid Program. Awards grants worth from $100 to $1,400 to residents for undergraduate study at in-state postsecondary institutions.

For further information, write Minnesota Higher Education Coordinating Commission, Suite 400, 550 Cedar Street, St. Paul, Minnesota 55101.

MISSISSIPPI

Academic Common Market. Allows residents to study at certain other Southern states at in-state tuition rates.

For further information, write Institutions of Higher Learning, Student Financial Aid Office, P.O. Box 2336, Jackson, Mississippi 39205.

MISSOURI

Missouri Student Grants. Awards grants worth from $70 to $1,500 to residents for full-time undergraduate study at in-state institutions. Recipients cannot major in theology or divinity.

For further information, write Missouri Department of Higher Education, P.O. Box 1437, Jefferson City, Missouri 65102.

MONTANA

Montana State Student Incentive Grants. Awards grants worth up to $600 to residents for full-time undergraduate study at in-state colleges or universities.

For further information, write Montana University System, 33 South Last Chance Gulch, Helena, Montana 59620.

NEBRASKA

Nebraska State Student Incentive Grants. Awards grants to residents for full-time undergraduate study at in-state institutions.

For further information, write Nebraska Coordinating Commission for Postsecondary Education, 301 Centennial Mall South, P.O. Box 95005, Lincoln, Nebraska 68509.

NEVADA

Nevada Student Incentive Grant Program. Awards grants to residents for undergraduate study at in-state institutions.

For further information, write University of Nevada System, 405 Marsh Avenue, Reno, Nevada 89509, or the institution that you wish to attend.

NEW HAMPSHIRE

New Hampshire Incentive Program. Awards grants worth from $100 to $1,500 to residents for full-time undergraduate study at in-state postsecondary institutions.

For further information, write New Hampshire Postsecondary Education Commission, 66 South Street, Concord, New Hampshire 03301.

NEW JERSEY

New Jersey Tuition Aid Grant Program. Awards grants worth from $100 to $1,400 to residents for full-time study at in-state colleges or at colleges in states that have reciprocity agreements with New Jersey.

Garden State Scholarship Program. Awards grants worth up to $500 to residents based on academic criteria and financial need for full-time undergraduate study.

New Jersey Educational Opportunity Fund Program. Awards grants to residents for full-time undergraduate study.

For further information, write Department of Higher Education, Office of Student Assistance, CN 540, Trenton, New Jersey 08625.

NEW MEXICO

New Mexico Student Incentive Grant Program. Awards grants worth up to $800 at public and $2,000 at private institutions to residents for in-state postsecondary study.

For further information, write Board of Educational Finance, Legislative-Executive Building, Room 201, Santa Fe, New Mexico 87503.

NEW YORK

New York Tuition Assistance Program. Awards grants worth up to $2,200 to residents for full-time study at in-state postsecondary schools. Students must enroll in degree programs at collegiate institutions; hospital programs in radiologic technology, radiography, or nursing; or certain two-year programs at registered business schools.

New York State Regents College Scholarship. Awards renewable scholarships worth $250 to residents based on either SAT or ACT scores for study at in-state postsecondary institutions.

Regents Scholarship in Cornell University. Awards grants worth from $100 to $1,000 to at least sixty residents planning to attend Cornell University.

New York State Regents Nursing Scholarship. Awards eight hundred renewable scholarships worth $250 to residents based either on SAT or ACT scores for study at in-state schools of nursing or colleges.

New York State also offers the following four grants to residents who are both academically and economically disadvantaged:

Educational Opportunity Program. Awards grants worth up to $2,200 for study at State University of New York (SUNY) two- and four-year colleges, including community colleges.

Higher Education Opportunity Program. Awards grants worth up to $1,500 for study at in-state private institutions.

Search for Elevation and Education through Knowledge. Awards grants worth up to $60 a week to residents of New York City for study at four-year City University of New York (CUNY) colleges.

College Discovery. Awards grants worth up to $60 a week to residents of New York City for study at one of the community colleges of the City University of New York.

New York State Parents' and Students' Saving Plan (PASS). Allows parents and other legally responsible relatives to contribute up to $750 a year per beneficiary to establish trust funds for future educational expenses and to claim contributions as deductions against New York State income taxes. Taxes are deferred until the beneficiary terminates his education. Then the student becomes liable for the deferred taxes, spread over a five-year period and based on his income tax bracket, not the parent's.

New York State Tuition Deduction Plan. Allows parents to claim a New York State income tax deduction of up to $1,000 for half of the tuition expenses of a full-time student enrolled at an in-state institution.

For further information, write New York State Higher Education Services Corporation, 99 Washington Avenue, Albany, New York 12255.

NORTH CAROLINA

North Carolina Student Incentive Grant (NCSIG) Program. Awards grants averaging $530 to residents for undergraduate study at in-state institutions.

North Carolina Legislative Tuition Grant (NCLTG) Program. Awards grants averaging $430 to residents for full-time study at in-state private colleges or universities.

For further information, write North Carolina State Education Assistance Authority, P.O. Box 2688, Chapel Hill, North Carolina 27514.

NORTH DAKOTA

North Dakota Student Financial Assistance Program. Awards grants worth up to $500 to residents for full-time undergraduate study at in-state institutions.

North Dakota Tuition Assistance Grant Program. Awards grants worth from $200 to $1,500 to residents for undergraduate study at Mary College, Jamestown College, Trinity Bible Institute, or Northwest Bible College.

North Dakota Nursing Scholarship/Loan Program. Provides loans to residents for the study of nursing. These loans may be cancelled if the nurse becomes employed in North Dakota.

For further information, write Student Financial Assistance Program, Tenth Floor, State Capitol, Bismarck, North Dakota 58505.

OHIO

Ohio Instructional Grant Program. Awards grants worth up to $900 at public ($2,250 private) schools in Ohio and Pennsylvania to residents for full-time undergraduate study. Eligible schools include colleges and universities, schools of nursing, and certain proprietary schools offering associate degrees.

Ohio Academic Scholarship Program. Awards one thousand renewable scholarships worth $1,000 to residents for full-time undergraduate study at in-state colleges or universities.

For further information, write Student Assistance Office, Ohio Board of Regents, 3600 State Office Tower, 30 East Broad Street, Columbus, Ohio 43215.

OKLAHOMA

Oklahoma Tuition Aid Grant Program. Awards grants worth up to $500 to residents for full-time undergraduate study at in-state institutions.

For further information, write Oklahoma State Regents for Higher Education, 500 Education Building, State Capitol Complex, Oklahoma City, Oklahoma 73105.

OREGON

Oregon Need Grant Program. Awards grants worth up to $1,100 to residents for full-time undergraduate study at in-state institutions. No awards may be made for the study of theology, divinity, or religion.

Oregon Cash Award Program. Awards grants worth up to $540 to residents based on both financial need and academic achievement for undergraduate study at in-state institutions.

For further information, write State Scholarship Commission, 1445 Willamette Street, Eugene, Oregon 97401.

PENNSYLVANIA

Pennsylvania State Higher Education Grant Program. Awards grants worth from $100 to $1,500 (in state) and from $100 to $600 (out of state) to residents for full-time undergraduate study. Out-of-state study is limited to accredited four-year colleges and universities located anywhere in the United States except New York State. In-state study includes certain business, trade, and technical schools in addition to colleges and universities.

For further information, write Pennsylvania Higher Education Assistance Agency, Towne House, Harrisburg, Pennsylvania 17102.

RHODE ISLAND

Rhode Island Higher Education Scholarship Program. Awards grants worth from $250 to $1,500 to residents based on both financial need and SAT scores for at least half-time undergraduate study at in-state or out-of-state postsecondary institutions.

Rhode Island Higher Education Grant Program. Awards grants worth from $250 to $1,500 to residents for at least half-time undergraduate study at in-state or out-of-state postsecondary institutions.

For further information, write Rhode Island Higher Education Assistance Authority, 274 Weybosset Street, Providence, Rhode Island 02903.

SOUTH CAROLINA

South Carolina State Student Incentive Grant. Awards grants worth up to $2,000 to residents for full-time undergraduate study at in-state institutions.

South Carolina Tuition Grants. Awards grants worth from $100 to $2,000 to residents for full-time undergraduate study at in-state private institutions.

State Grants for Out-of-State Study. Awards grants worth up to $500 to residents for out-of-state study in majors not offered in state. These grants are not based upon financial need.

For further information, write Commission on Higher Education, 1429 Senate Street, Columbia, South Carolina 29201.

SOUTH DAKOTA

South Dakota Student Incentive Grant Program. Awards grants worth from $100 to $2,000 to residents for at least half-time study at in-state institutions.

For further information, write Education and Cultural Affairs, Office of the Secretary, Richard F. Kneip Building, Pierre, South Dakota 57501.

TENNESSEE

Tennessee Student Assistance Award Program. Awards grants worth from $100 to $2,000 to residents for undergraduate study at in-state institutions.

For further information, write Tennessee Student Assistance Corporation, B-3 Capitol Towers, Suite 9, Nashville, Tennessee 37219.

TEXAS

Tuition Equalization Grant. Awards grants worth up to $1,328 to residents for at least half-time study at in-state private colleges and universities.

Tuition Equalization Grant/State Student Incentive Grant. Awards grants worth up to $1,000 using the same criteria as the Tuition Equalization Grant. A student can receive awards from both of these programs.

Texas Public Educational Grant. Awards grants to students attending in-state public institutions. No more than 10 percent of the funds may go to nonresident students.

Texas Public Educational/State Student Incentive Grant. Awards grants worth up to $2,000 to students attending in-state public institutions. No more than 10 percent of the funds may go to nonresident students.

Applications for all of these programs are available

through participating institutions. For further information, write Coordinating Board, P.O. Box 12788, Capitol Station, Austin, Texas 78711.

UTAH

State Student Incentive Grant. Awards grants worth up to $2,000 to residents attending in-state colleges or universities.

For further information, write Utah State Board of Regents, 807 East South Temple, Suite 204, Salt Lake City, Utah 84102.

VERMONT

Vermont Incentive Grants Program. Awards grants worth up to $2,150 to residents for full-time undergraduate study at in-state or out-of-state institutions.

Private Tuition Differential Grant Program. Awards grants worth as much as $1,100 to residents for full-time undergraduate study at in-state private institutions.

Senatorial Scholarship Program. Awards grants worth as much as $300 to residents for study at postsecondary institutions, in state if possible.

For further information, write Vermont Student Assistance Corporation, 5 Burlington Square, Burlington, Vermont 05401.

VIRGINIA

Virginia College Scholarship Assistance Program. Awards grants worth from $200 to $600 to residents for full-time undergraduate study at in-state colleges or universities.

Virginia Tuition Assistance Grant Program. Awards grants worth up to $700 to residents for full-time undergraduate study at in-state private colleges or universities.

Commonwealth Incentive Grant Program. Awards nonrenewable grants worth $1,000 to "other race" residents enrolled full-time at traditionally white or black four-year public colleges or universities in Virginia.

Eastern Shore Tuition Assistance Program. Awards grants worth $700 to residents of Northampton or Accomack counties who are juniors or seniors and who commute to the University of Maryland/Eastern Shore or Salisbury State College.

For further information, write State Council of Higher Education for Virginia, 101 North Fourteenth Street, James Monroe Building, Richmond, Virginia 23219.

WASHINGTON

Need Grant Program. Awards grants to residents for full-time undergraduate study at in-state institutions. Applicants cannot pursue a degree in theology.

Tuition Waiver Program. Waives tuition for needy or disadvantaged residents enrolled full time at in-state public two- and four-year colleges and universities. Application is automatic when a student applies for financial aid at the college of his choice.

Paul L. Fowler Memorial Scholarship Program. Awards five renewable scholarships worth $1,500 to residents for full-time undergraduate study at accredited colleges or universities anywhere in the world.

For further information, write Council for Postsecondary Education, 908 East Fifth Avenue, EW-11, Olympia, Washington 98504.

WEST VIRGINIA

West Virginia Higher Education Grant Program. Awards grants worth from $200 to $1,810 to residents for full-time undergraduate study at approved universities or colleges located in West Virginia, Pennsylvania, or New Jersey. Applicants must submit ACT scores to demonstrate academic potential as well as financial need.

For further information, write West Virginia Higher Education Grant Program, 950 Kanawha Boulevard East, Charleston, West Virginia 25301.

WISCONSIN

Wisconsin Higher Education Grants (WHEG). Awards grants worth up to $1,800 to residents for at least half-time undergraduate study at a University of Wisconsin system school or a vocational technical school.

Wisconsin Tuition Grant Program. Awards grants worth up to $2,000 to residents for at least half-time undergraduate study at in-state private colleges or vocational schools.

WHEG Component—Talent Incentive Program (TIP). Awards grants to very needy residents enrolled as undergraduates at in-state institutions.

Minnesota-Wisconsin Reciprocity Agreement. Waives extra out-of-state tuition at public-institutions.

For further information, write Higher Educational Aids Board, 137 East Wilson Street, Madison, Wisconsin 53702.

WYOMING

State Student Incentive Grants. Awards grants worth up to $2,000 to undergraduate residents enrolled at in-state institutions.

County Commissioners Scholarship. Awards funds worth full tuition to undergraduate residents at in-state public colleges.

For further information, write Community College Commission, 1720 Carey Avenue, Boyd Building, Fifth Floor, Cheyenne, Wyoming 82002.

COLLEGE PROGRAMS

The educational institution the student attends could be another important source of aid, especially if it's private. Famous universities such as the Ivies, M.I.T., Stanford, or the University of Chicago offer enormous amounts of aid to supplement the federal and state. A needy student capable of acceptance by this kind of institution would be foolish not to apply. Some families, especially those with severe need, are dumbfounded at the size of the awards they receive. Under the right circumstances, these can be the least expensive places to attend college. Less affluent colleges have lower tuitions, but they also have less to offer in financial aid. They're also more likely to target their aid toward candidates they really want.

PRIVATE SCHOLARSHIPS

There are literally thousands of private scholarships available from corporations, religious denominations, organizations, and foundations. The vast majority of these use financial need as the key criterion, but frequently they specify what college major must be selected, which company or organization a parent must work for or belong to, what race or religion the student must be, or make other requirements that an applicant may or may not be able to fulfill. Occasionally an applicant has to compete by writing an essay, taking a test, or describing his achievements in school. Although many of these awards are relatively modest in comparison to the cost of higher education, some are quite lucrative. Because all of them require applications, occasionally lengthy, a student who plans to pursue several should be prepared to devote time to the process.

Since there are so many of these scholarships offered, determining which are most suitable is a problem. Recently several companies have begun to offer computer searches for scholarships. An applicant to one of these companies completes a form describing his activities and intended major, plus family information such as race, organizations they belong to, companies they work for, and military background. Using this information, the computer searches for appropriate scholarships for this applicant. Since the computer is constantly updated, its bank of information is kept current.

Theoretically this is a terrific idea, but in practice the results haven't been impressive. For instance, I've seen returns that listed ROTC or coop as suggestions. One listed SEOG, even though it's a campus-based program that can't be applied for directly. A student who applied later than he should have received eighteen suggestions, seven of which were unusable since their deadlines had already passed—according to the very computer that suggested them. Evidently this computer was programmed to list deadlines for applications, but it wasn't instructed to stop recommending scholarships after the deadlines had passed.

Also, the information that an applicant receives is limited to the bare essentials: a computer printout of the name of the scholarship, the address, the amount of the award, and the closing date for applications. Finally, these computer searches are not cheap. Most cost about $45 to $65.

If a reader wishes to utilize a computer search, probably the best is Scholarship Search, Applications Center, 1775 Broadway, New York, New York 10102.

Personally, I prefer a faster method that costs much less. *Financial Aids for Higher Education Catalog*, by Oreon Keeslar, allows quick location of the identical scholarships listed by a computer. Its Program Finder asks the reader a series of questions: Are you the child of an Armed Forces veteran, or of someone now in the service? Are you a war orphan? Are you a member of one of these clubs or organizations? Are you a member of one of these churches?

Besides these questions page numbers are listed so the student can turn directly to descriptions of the appropriate scholarships. This is an excellent reference book and it is in most guidance offices and libraries, so readers should be able to locate a copy easily.

Another good source is the *College Blue Book,* which should also be available in most libraries and guidance offices. It consists of five volumes, one of which is devoted to scholarships. Unlike Keeslar's book, the *College Blue Book* confines itself to two categories: college majors and scholarships for minorities. It's quite complete in both these categories.

In addition to these sources of information, Black students should contact the national or local offices of the National Scholarship Service and Fund for Negro Students (NSSFNS). This service is designed to provide Blacks with financial information and advice for higher education. For particulars, write The National Scholarship Service and Fund for Negro Students, 562 Third Street, Brooklyn, New York 11215.

NATIONAL MERIT SCHOLARSHIP PROGRAM

One program with which everyone should be familiar is the National Merit. This program is based on the results of the PSAT/NMSQT test, which is offered only in October each year. To be eligible to compete in the program, a student must be a junior in high school or in the process of graduating early. Out of approximately one million students who take the test every year, about 15,000 become semifinalists. At least a thousand of these semifinalists become National Merit Scholars and receive $1,000, nonrenewable awards toward college expenses. Also, corporations and colleges may sponsor other high scorers, who become corporate-sponsored or college-sponsored Merit Scholars.

In addition, if a Black student taking the PSAT/NMSQT marks a space on his answer sheet that asks whether he wishes to be considered for the National Achievement Scholarship Program for Outstanding Negro Students, he will be included in this program as well as the National Merit. Similar to the National Merit Program, the National Achievement Program offers $1,000 scholarships plus corporate- and college-sponsored scholarships.

Further information about these programs can be obtained through high school guidance offices.

LOCAL SCHOLARSHIPS

One last source of financial aid remains, local scholarships. These scholarships rarely reach any national source of scholarship information such as computer searches or the Keeslar book since they are intended solely for students from a certain locale, frequently a single high school. Sometimes high schools receive donations or bequests, or local chapters of the Daughters of the American Revolution or Knights of Columbus decide to offer scholarships. A high school normally announces these scholarships plus other scholarship notices from colleges or national organizations through bulletin boards and collections of scholarship information in the guidance office. Since one or more flyers arrive at a guidance office almost daily, it's too expensive for a high school to mail all of these announcements home to parents.

Consequently, there's no substitute for a student who's alert. Some students are almost completely oblivious to all written information, while others watch for announcements and stop at the guidance office occasionally to peruse what has arrived. A student who walks around in a dream world would probably miss some opportunities.

7

HOW TO APPLY FOR
FINANCIAL AID

Most students will want to apply for financial aid from three sources: the federal government, the state government, and the college. Technically, it isn't necessary to apply to all three of these sources, but to receive aid from a college a student must have applied for federal and state aid and to receive state aid he must have applied for federal. Consequently, most students are locked in to applying to all three.

Frequently, there are several ways of accomplishing this, and it could become confusing to someone who has never applied. If the following explanation still leaves you in a quandary or problems arise as you fill in the form or forms, talk to a guidance counselor or a college financial-aid officer. They can respond to your specific questions.

FEDERAL AID

Federal aid can be applied for in many ways. Probably the easiest is to include the federal request with a form that can also be used by a college and/or the state. For instance, the Financial Aid Form (FAF) of the College Scholarship Service and the Family Financial Statement (FFS) of American College Testing can be used to apply for federal aid, and they are also used by many colleges and states. Therefore, if a student applied to a college requiring an FAF and the state also required the FAF, that one form could be used to apply for aid from all three sources. An applicant would list all three sources of aid as recipients and mail that one form to the College Scholarship Service if it's an FAF or to American College Testing if it's an FFS. There is also a federal form called the AFSA (Application for Federal Student Aid) if someone wanted to apply for federal aid only.

STATE AID

The following states use the FAF. Consequently, a student who lives in one of these states can probably fill out this one form to apply for all three sources of aid.

Alaska	Maine
Connecticut	Maryland
Florida	Massachusetts
Georgia	New Hampshire
Hawaii	New Jersey
Idaho	Oregon
Indiana	Rhode Island
Iowa	West Virginia
Kentucky	Wisconsin

The following states use the FFS. Consequently, a student in one of these states can probably fill out this one form to apply for all three sources of aid.

Arkansas
Kansas
Minnesota
North Dakota (plus another state application)

The following states use either the FAF or the FFS, whichever is preferred by the college to which the student has applied:

Illinois (also accepts AFSA)

Michigan

Missouri

Montana (college or university, FAF; vocational/ technical school, FFS)

Oklahoma

Tennessee

The following states recommend that eligible students apply through the institution they plan to attend. Presumably, since most institutions use the FAF or FFS, students would complete one of these two forms.

Alabama	North Carolina
Arizona	Ohio
Colorado	South Carolina
Delaware	South Dakota
District of Columbia	Texas
Louisiana	Utah
Mississippi	Vermont
Nebraska	Washington
Nevada	Wyoming
New Mexico	

California requires a Student Aid Application for California (SAAC), which is very similar to the FAF and is in fact processed by the College Scholarship Service. This same form can be used to apply for federal and college aid.

New York requires a Student Payment Application to apply for its Tuition Assistance Program (TAP), and there are other applications necessary for other state programs. Another form such as the FAF or FFS can be used to apply for federal and college aid.

Pennsylvania requires a combined state and federal aid form, and the FAF or FFS can be used to apply for college aid.

Virginia requires an FAF, but additional applications may be necessary to apply for certain of its programs.

COLLEGE AID

Each college can establish whatever it desires in the form of applications. Generally, most require either the FAF or the FFS, but some may only require that the student apply for federal and state aid. Colleges that require merely a state and federal application for aid usually lack large aid programs of their own and base their awards on the results of the federal and/or state analysis. On the other hand, colleges with sizable aid programs will sometimes require the completion of one of their own applications for aid in addition to an FAF or FFS.

OTHER SOURCES OF AID

Private scholarship programs sponsored by organizations such as corporations, American Legions, or womens' clubs usually include requests for financial information on their application. If the program is a large one, it may request that applicants file an FAF or FFS with a local college, which determines applicants' needs as a service to the sponsor. This process is considerably better than when sponsors perform the analysis themselves, but it's not widely used. Sponsors delight in performing private analyses, even when the results are not nearly as scientific or equitable as those performed by professionals. Apparently the psychological satisfaction of having been a part of the decision-making process is a necessary complement to their philanthropy.

I hope this explanation of how to apply for aid has clarified the situation. The crucial factor to keep in mind is that the three main sources of aid (the federal government, the state, and the institution itself) must be covered. If you think through who will receive the results of each application for aid that you file, you should be safe.

All of the described applications are available through high school guidance offices and college financial aid offices. Pick them up in state, though. Many states have personalized their FAFs and FFSs. If a Massachusetts resident picks up an FAF while visiting a college in Rhode Island, the results of his FAF will be sent automatically to the Rhode Island Higher Education Assistance Authority.

POINTS TO REMEMBER IN COMPLETING APPLICATIONS

Many mechanical problems can arise in filing for financial aid. Here are a few things to keep in mind since they have caused problems in the past:

1. Every applicant for aid needs a social security number.
2. Applicants must print legibly.
3. All required signatures must be included.
4. No requested answer may be omitted. If the proper response is zero, enter zero. You cannot leave an answer blank or enter N/A.

5. Fill in numerical answers from the right, not the left. For instance, write ☐ ☐ ⑤ ⓪, not ⑤ ⓪ ☐ ☐, if you want to enter $50. That second response might be taken as $5,000. Since the FAF doesn't use boxes, this problem is mostly associated with the FFS.

6. Enter whole numbers only, never cents. Write $50, not $50.26

7. If you complete more than one application, be certain they agree. For instance, if you complete one application in January and the next in February, the amounts in your checking and savings accounts could have changed, and this might cause problems even though you have completed each application accurately on the day you worked on it. It's best to xerox your applications and make any second or third agree with the first, assuming no dramatic change has occurred in your financial situation.

8. If for some reason you aren't able to complete your tax return when you need to file an aid application, complete the application using estimated figures. If the actual tax return figures differ from those that you filed in your application for aid, you will have to correct your original estimates.

9. Try to avoid duplication. If you list the federal government as a recipient of an FAF or FFS, don't also file an AFSA.

10. Incomplete applications: If a student using an FAF or FFS to apply for a Pell Grant receives inquiries from the intermediate processor and Pell Grant, possibly because his application was incomplete or illegible, that student must respond to both inquiries. The agreement between Pell Grant and the intermediate processors covers only the transmission of original data. Any additional data will

not be sent to Pell Grant by the College Scholarship Service or American College Testing.

11. Changes in an application: A change in circumstances that would affect an FAF or FFS application can be communicated to the processor by letter. If the student has used one of these forms to apply for federal aid, the change in circumstances must also be communicated to Pell Grant. Generally, this can be done by signing and making the correction on the SAR and sending it to Federal Student Aid Programs, Box 92440, Los Angeles, California 90009–2440. If you write, be sure to include your name, date of birth, and social security number.

    After applying, if a major change occurs due to death, disability, divorce or separation, or unemployment of more than ten weeks, a Special Condition Application for Federal Student Aid must be filed. Remember that a Special Condition can be filed as late as March 15 of the school year for which the application is intended. Consequently, if a parent died or lost his job, his child could apply for aid based on the family's estimated future earning rather than the previous year's actual and receive aid for the current school year even if most of it is already completed.

12. Most applications for aid cannot be filed until January 1 for the school year beginning the following September. Some high competitive colleges, however, will send early decision applicants an Early Version of the FAF, which may be filed in the fall using estimated figures. These colleges can then give students estimates of what they will receive in aid. Later these applicants will have to file corrected returns when the final figures become available. These Early Versions are available

only through participating colleges. Also, some private scholarship plans that use their own applications rather than the FAF or FFS may request returns before January 1. But generally, January is the month for filing applications for aid. Applicants who delay too long will find that all aid has already been committed.

If you have problems with your applications, the best person you can talk to is the college financial-aid officer. In addition, if you have a question concerning the progress of your Pell Grant application (whether it has been received or when it will be processed, for instance), you can call (213) 820-2800 (not a toll-free number). Wait at least ten weeks before calling. For general questions concerning federal aid or applications, call (800) 638-6700 for the mainland forty-eight states, District of Columbia, and Puerto Rico, except that in Maryland the number is (800) 492-6602. Both of these are toll-free numbers. For those who prefer to write for information, brochures, or applications, the address is Federal Student Financial Assistance, P.O. Box 84, Washington, D.C. 20044.

III

Beyond Financial Aid

8

COLLEGE COMPARISON SHOPPING

While this section could benefit any family, those that qualify for little or no aid and who can't afford a Cadillac or a Mercedes either probably have the most to gain: in other words, much of the middle class. In this chapter and the ones that follow I will outline every means I know to reduce college expenses apart from obtaining financial aid.

Ironically, my experience has been that many families that agonize over the cost of college send their children to institutions that they honestly feel are beyond their means. They agonize, they worry, they complain, but they pay. Somehow colleges are different from the rest of the world. One is expected to disregard monetary considerations in their selection. Families that wouldn't dream of purchasing a car or a refrigerator without searching for the best buy (which isn't necessarily the one that's cheapest), send their children to colleges costing many times as much with scarcely a thought as to the alternatives. It's simply the thing to do. But is it wise? Let's think the unthinkable and examine the cost of college from an economic viewpoint.

First, have you ever considered what it means to spend, say, $10,000 more than is necessary for a college education? Well, since that $10,000 would have been saved otherwise, we're really talking about $10,000 worth of savings, which is far different from $10,000 worth of earnings. Earnings are ephemeral. All but a small portion of earnings are taxed or frittered away. In America we save either 5.6 percent of our earnings, according to the *Wall Street Journal*, or 6.3 percent, according to *Forbes* magazine. Even if we take the larger figure, a typical family would have to earn $158,730 in order to replace that $10,000 of savings. Let's assume dramatically better savings, 10 percent a year. At that rate, it would take $100,000 of earnings for a family to recoup the missing $10,000. How long does it take you to earn $100,000? Remember, this discussion concerns an *extra* $10,000 in savings, not merely $10,000 in savings.

Some families spend much more than an extra $10,000. I've seen "no-need" scholarships worth as much as full tuition go begging because the students who qualified for them weren't interested. Just recently I saw one for full tuition go unfilled. It was to a state-related university, a very fine school that typically draws from the top two-fifths of high school classes and has average SATs of about 1000. It's not Harvard or Yale, but it's a fine school, far better than the vast majority. Those students who were interested in this scholarship couldn't qualify academically, and those who could qualify had their sights set on more prestigious institutions. Some of the parents of those students who rejected this scholarship will wind up paying an additional $20,000 to $40,000 for their children's degrees. Some of these students themselves will pay more, too, since they'll have to take out loans during college whereas loans might have been avoided by accepting the scholarship.

Let's consider debt. Many college students will graduate owing money, especially if they attend graduate school. Medical-school students, especially, acquire heavy debts. Recently I read of one who owed $60,000.

What are the ramifications of this? Don't young people face sufficient problems without starting life in debt? Aren't many college graduates having trouble even finding jobs? When they find them, don't they begin at relatively modest salaries? Traditionally, haven't people just starting out in life needed expensive goods? A home? A car? Furniture? A refrigerator? A television set? Won't college debt exacerbate these problems?

In recent years a number of articles have been written about the prolongation of adolescence. Parents today frequently find themselves still assisting their children even after they've graduated from college and are supposedly independent. Sometimes parents help out by buying things for them. Often they lend money for a deposit on a home. Occasionally they finance new college degrees because the original ones weren't sufficiently career-oriented. One way or another, in many families adolescence has been extended until the children are well into their twenties or even thirties. Parents who think that their problems will end once their children graduate are dreaming.

It's foolish for a student to acquire debt, a negative dowry, unless it's absolutely imperative. Students sometimes become so excited about college that they forget that there's life afterward.

Sometimes their parents do the same thing. Recently a friend of mine related the story of a neighbor who had just finished financing three college educations when her husband died. Now she's worried about what she'll live on. And she can't ask for a recount on financial aid because they misjudged her husband's life expectancy.

Each family must rationalize its economic decisions in its own way. Remember, as you read the suggestions in part 3, that the perfect plan for saving money probably does not exist. Life is a series of compromises. If price is important, then you may have to accept some disadvantages. If you're unwilling to accept any, then perhaps price isn't really that important after all. Outside the world of financial aid, there's no such thing as a free lunch.

STATE-OWNED OR STATE-RELATED COLLEGES AND UNIVERSITIES

Attending a public rather than a private institution is obviously the most popular means of saving money. State colleges are considerably cheaper than private ones, and this option is the easiest to understand and to utilize, since nobody has to compete for anything or perform any esoteric maneuvering. You merely pay relatively inexpensive tuition as a resident of the state or community.

In spite of the fine public educations that are available, there are occasional drawbacks to this option. First, although state systems of higher education normally offer almost every imaginable major somewhere in their systems, the selection may be limited. Take astronomy, for instance. *Lovejoy's College Guide* lists Penn State as the only state college in Pennsylvania offering it as a major (at University Park and three of its two-year branches). But astronomy is also offered by Bryn Mawr College, Drexel University, Haverford College, Lycoming College, and Villanova University. By including private institutions, a Pennsylvania student would have a choice of two of the most prestigious colleges in the country, a women's college, a university that specializes in work/study plans, a Catholic university, and a small college located in a beautiful area of the Pocono Mountains. Some of these alternatives could prove tempting.

Size and the composition of the student body could be further considerations. Most state colleges, especially the main branches, which tend to be the crown jewels of the state systems, are quite large compared to private institutions. Moreover, the vast majority of their students come from within the state. All state colleges charge the out-of-state student more than the in-state student, which tends to discourage out-of-state applications; and some of the popular ones (such as the College of William and Mary and the University of North Carolina at Chapel Hill) severely limit the number of out-of-state students that they will accept. Private colleges do exactly the opposite. They encourage applications from students who live in other states and even foreign countries because they feel that a heterogeneous student body is in itself a learning experience for their students.

Another aspect of the public versus the private college is admittedly quite subjective. State colleges try to deliver quality educations as economically as possible to large numbers of students. A few of our very famous private institutions, however, spend considerably more money per student and presumably are able to offer finer educations (to those students who take advantage of what is offered; the student is an active ingredient in the learning process). Take a look at these figures:

Public Schools	Approx. no. full-time undergraduates	Student-to-faculty ratio	No. volumes in library	No. volumes per full-time undergraduate
Ohio State Univ. at Columbus	38,000	16 to 1	3,500,000	92
SUNY at Stony Brook	10,100	15 to 1	1,180,000	117
Univ. of Arizona	18,500	22 to 1	1,275,000	69
UCLA	19,000	17 to 1	4,000,000	211
Univ. of Florida	22,900	20 to 1	2,000,000	87
Univ. of Massachusetts at Amherst	18,300	18 to 1	2,400,000	131
Univ. of Wisconsin at Madison	24,000	16 to 1	3,300,000	138
Private Schools				
Claremont Coll./Pomona Coll.	1,350	11 to 1	1,000,000	741
Duke Univ.	6,600	9 to 1	3,000,000	455
MIT	4,600	5 to 1	1,600,000	348
Swarthmore College	1,300	9 to 1	552,000	425
Univ. of Chicago	2,700	8 to 1	3,500,000	1,296
Vassar Coll.	2,200	11 to 1	505,00	230
Yale Univ.	5,200	7 to 1	8,000,000	1,538

In regard to these statistics, it should be noted that the student-to-teacher ratio can be misleading. Most schools have some faculty members who teach only part-time, for instance. The honest way to count a person who teaches a partial schedule is to label him a half or quarter of a full-time teacher, whatever fraction he teaches. Some schools do it this way, but others fudge. Even so, it is certain that there are substantial differences among these colleges in regard to their student-to-faculty ratios.

These statistics tell only part of the story. Not only does a school such as Yale have more professors in proportion to the number of students than a state school, but it's a pretty safe bet that Yale's are better paid and, on the average, more distinguished. Also, no comparison was attempted involving the physical plants of these institutions. Can you imagine the scientific equipment MIT must have? All in all, some private schools must spend much more per pupil than public schools. This difference is likely to remain, since the public would never stand for the taxes necessary to support such expensive educations.

On the other hand, although a fair comparison between private and state institutions was attempted, even so the private colleges listed are outstanding and not at all representative of private colleges in general. Moreover, their tuitions and other costs are among the highest in the nation, so they're outstanding in that respect too.

The vast majority of private colleges are no better than public ones, and frequently they aren't as good. In addition, the plight of private colleges has been steadily deteriorating since they are caught in a financial bind. Inflation is sending their costs soaring; but when they try to pass these costs along through higher tuition, fewer students apply, since public colleges are so much cheaper. Consequently, many private colleges are trying to hold the line on costs: letting student-to-teacher ratios rise, purchasing fewer books for the library, spending less on scientific equipment, eliminating some of the unusual courses that relatively few students take. In the years ahead, as the number of college-bound students drops because of the smaller numbers of college-age Americans, many private colleges will close their doors. Generally speaking, the private sector has many more problems than the public.

All in all, a state college represents good value, and the advantages of this option are not easily matched elsewhere. There may be certain private colleges that offer more than public ones (for a higher price), but there are many more that offer no more, or even less (for a higher price).

One last consideration regarding public versus private colleges is that large areas of our country lack a healthy diversity of private institutions. In these areas, unless a family is willing to send a child a considerable distance, there isn't much of an alternative to public education.

Let's compare regions. I live in suburban Philadelphia. Within a half hour's drive of my home are four of the most prestigious private institutions in the country: Bryn Mawr College, Haverford College, Swarthmore College, and the University of Pennsylvania. Name a private institution in Arizona that even remotely resembles one of those four. There isn't any. Arizona has the University of Arizona and Arizona State, both large state institutions. There are a few smaller state schools and community colleges too, but almost nothing in the private sector. There's just one traditional, four-year, fully accredited, private college.

Can you name an outstanding private institution in New Mexico? What about Oklahoma? Nebraska? The Dakotas? Wyoming? Idaho?

Here's another measure. Most of the high-quality colleges and universities have chapters of Phi Beta Kappa, and reading a list of these institutions is like reading a *Who's Who* of colleges. In Pennsylvania, fourteen private colleges or universities have such chapters (plus three others that are state-owned or state-related). Here is a list of states in which there isn't a single private institution that has such a chapter: Arizona, Arkansas, Idaho, Kansas, Mississippi, Montana, Nebraska, Nevada, New Mexico, North Dakota, Oklahoma, South Dakota, Utah, and Wyoming.

Some states have only one: Oregon has Reed College, Washington has Whitman College, and Louisiana has Tulane University.

There's a reason for this phenomenon: the establishment of land-grant colleges and universities. When this country was still spreading westward, the federal government passed the Morrill, or Land-Grant, Act of 1862. This Act granted land to each state, the land to be sold and the proceeds used to endow colleges and universities for agriculture and the mechanical arts. While this widely praised Act has accomplished much that has been good for our nation, one of its unfortunate byproducts was that people stopped establishing private institutions as they moved westward.

It's fascinating to trace the pattern. The Northeast has the heaviest concentration of private schools, and they become sparser west of Ohio. There is good selection until one gets a little west of Chicago, but from there on it becomes pretty sporadic. The South never had as large a selection as the North, but it becomes even smaller the farther one moves away from the states on the Eastern Seaboard. The two exceptions to this pattern are California, which has a wide range of private institutions, and Texas, which has quite a few choices, many of them very reasonable financially. Otherwise, the American West does not offer a wide diversity of private colleges and universities.

In summary, it looks as though public education is a good choice anywhere, and the most logical option in some places, unless one is willing to travel.

PUBLIC COLLEGES OF OTHER STATES

It is usually possible to attend a state college as an out-of-state student more cheaply than it is to attend private colleges. State colleges add a charge called "additional out-of-state tuition," and while this frequently makes them more expensive than in-state colleges, they still remain cheaper than the private. Typically, state colleges charge about an extra $1,500 a year, but there are wide variations. Some charge well under $1,000 extra, while others tack on over $3,000. Even within the same state there are differences. Generally, the main branch of a state university charges more than its branches or other state colleges.

The key factor seems to be how each state views out-of-state students. From what I've observed, states popular with tourists tend to have high additional costs, presumably because they fear that that their attractions would draw too many out-of-staters. A few others keep their additional costs amazingly low, but perhaps I had better not identify them, because they probably wouldn't remain low once they received some publicity. Anyone interested can easily research the situation in a book called *The College Cost Book*, published yearly by the College Board. High-school guidance offices should have copies.

An out-of-state public institution can certainly widen an applicant's list of attractive colleges and geographical locales, but otherwise it has many of the same qualities as the in-state choice. If a Pennsylvanian goes to a branch of SUNY, he'll be with mostly New Yorkers. Moreover, none of the state colleges is religiously oriented, and, regardless of state, they tend to be large. Nevertheless, some of the state college systems are undeniably superior to others, so a wide choice is desirable.

Keep in mind that state colleges discriminate in terms of admissions as well as tuition. Again the philosophy varies from state to state. The University of Virginia is extremely difficult for an out-of-state student to enter, while the University of Vermont isn't nearly as discriminatory. Vermont charges high extra tuition once you get there, though.

One perennial question concerns state residency. If you are a resident of one state but want to attend a public college in another state, how can a switch of state residencies be effected? The answer is: not too easily.

The barriers are, first, that most states require a year's residency before a student is considered in-state, and, second, that most states consider a student's residence to be his parent's address as long as his parents are supporting him. The second requirement is frequently decisive unless the student's parents actually move to the other state. If a student wishes to establish residency, his best bet is probably to become an independent student, a category we'll discuss later.

To ensure that applicants and their families are in-state residents, public colleges normally ask such questions as where they last voted, where their cars are registered, where they're licensed to drive, and where they pay state income taxes. It's hard to cheat on these questions unless there's an unusual family situation (divorce, separation, student living with relatives, etc.) or the student delays college for a year or so.

LESS EXPENSIVE COLLEGES WITH HONORS PROGRAMS

One of the unfortunate facts of life is that, usually, the better a college is, the more expensive it is. That's because the things that make a college outstanding happen to be expensive. When you cut class size, hire famous professors, purchase the latest laboratory equipment, provide better facilities, and beautify the campus, you improve a college. You also send the expenses of that college through the roof. Consequently, parents sometimes face the dilemma of dissipating the family fortune or watching the apple of their eyes receive a more conventional education. We have a better idea, at least for a good student.

Many colleges have honors programs that were established to attract superior students. By isolating these students from the others, the college can give them special attention that will make their educations comparable to those offered by more famous, and expensive, institutions. Let's take an example:

	Princeton Univ.		Univ. of South Carolina (main campus)	
Room, board, tuition, fees (1982–83)	$11,530		$2,772 in-state $4,052 out-of-state	
Approx. no. of full-time undergraduates	4,500		18,000	
Student-to-faculty ratio	7 to 1		19 to 1	
Size of library (volumes)	3,000,000		1,700,000	
SAT scores of freshmen (fall 1979)	Verbal	Math	Verbal	Math
700–800	19%	25%	1%	2%
600–699	35%	50%	6%	13%
500–599	30%	20%	19%	32%
400–499	15%	4%	46%	39%
300–399	1%	1%	27%	14%
200–299	0%	0%	1%	0%

Obviously there are substantial differences between these institutions. First, Princeton *costs* more than four times as much as South Carolina for an in-state student and almost three times as much for an out-of-state student. Second, Princeton apparently *spends* considerably more per student than South Carolina. Third, Princeton's program is designed for a different kind of student than is South Carolina's. For instance, Princeton professors teaching English composition expect finer papers from their students than South Carolina professors: Professors adjust to their students, as well as vice versa.

Apparently, an upper-middle-class family that won't qualify for aid lacks a good choice at either of these schools. If they send their child to Princeton, it'll cost an arm and a leg; and if they send him to South Carolina, he might not receive as challenging an education as he deserves. But is this a fair conclusion? Let's take a closer look at how South Carolina handles talented students.

In 1978 the University of South Carolina reestablished South Carolina College, which was the original name of the university at its founding in 1801, as the honors college of the university. The objective of the university was to provide a small liberal-arts college for highly motivated students within the confines of a major university. In this way honors students would have the intimacy and challenge of the College combined with the facilities and breadth of course offerings provided by the university.

South Carolina College professors include the university's most outstanding teachers and scholars, many of whom otherwise teach only in the graduate school or on the upper-division undergraduate level. South Carolina College students have a voice in their selection. Since average class size is fifteen, most classes operate as seminars emphasizing discussion and special projects rather than the usual lectures and multiple-choice examinations. Here are some details from Carolina College literature:

One American government class was organized like a graduate seminar, where students' grades were based primarily on two in-depth, research-based oral reports and discussion of other students' reports. In another class, the instructor, who was writing a text-book, made copies of each chapter as he completed it and distributed them to his class as a basis for discussion, thereby affording the students the opportunity to observe scholarly activity in progress.

In addition to the courses in the College, students have access to the rest of the university. This becomes increasingly important each year as students progress in their majors and need more unusual courses, but these classes are usually small also. The large classes of the university are the introductory courses, and these are all duplicated by the College in small group-ings. Typically, honors students take about half of their courses through the College. Graduating students receive their degrees from the university, with honors from the College. All honors courses are noted on the students' academic transcripts.

Admission to the College is subjective, but in general the admissions officers want students who score 1200 or higher on the SAT, graduate in the top 10 percent of their classes, and show writing ability. Transfers should offer a grade-point average of at least 3.5 in substantial courses; but if they transferred after more than one year of college work, they would have difficulty meeting the honors college requirements before graduation from the university.

Since South Carolina College costs the university several thousand dollars more per year per student, all students accepted by the College receive de facto scholarships. In addition, however, these students can apply for financial aid on a need basis and can compete for academic scholarships. South Carolina residents who score 1200 or better on the SAT and rank high in their classes can compete for fifteen Carolina Scholars Awards worth $2,000 each per year. All students who score 1200 or better on the SAT and rank in the top 10 percent of their classes can compete for one hundred Alumni Scholars Awards worth $500 each per year. Students with outstanding credentials are eligible for Trustees Scholars Awards worth full tuition or President's Scholars Awards worth half tuition. The university also sponsors National Merit Scholars for a minimum of $250 per year, although up to $2,000 a year is possible on the basis of financial need. Finally, various colleges and departments also award scholarships to entering freshmen or continuing students in their disciplines who have superior records.

Well, how does South Carolina look now for an outstanding student? With a special program such as this the difference between a Princeton and a South Carolina isn't quite as clear-cut. For the College South Carolina wants students who are in the top 10 percent of their high-school classes and score over 1200 on the SAT. That's comparable to Princeton's standards. South Carolina guarantees small classes for honor students. Will they be even smaller at Princeton? South Carolina gives the cream of its faculty to the Honors College. Is the average Princeton professor superior to the very best from South Carolina?

There are many of these programs at all kinds of colleges and universities. The better programs certainly remove much of the academic incentive for sending a child to an expensive college. Is Princeton really worth $30,000 or $40,000 more than South Carolina? From a purely educational standpoint, this difference is hard to rationalize. When parents are willing to pay that much extra, we're really talking about reputation, not education. That's a lot to pay for a name.

There's another point that hasn't been considered yet. One doesn't make a splash at a Princeton easily. Many of the students at famous colleges would be much better off as big fish in small ponds, rather than vice versa. At less impressive colleges, students start off as somebody just because they are in the honors program. Frequently, they even end up on college committees, such as admissions or curriculum, and have experiences that they'd never have had otherwise. Even if we forget finances, a program like South Carolina's might be the wisest choice for certain students.

Ideally, if a student pursues this option, he should try to combine it with a no-need scholarship. He will start with a less expensive college and cut his costs still further with the scholarship. Even without the scholarship, however, much money can be saved by simply attending a cheaper college that has an honors program. Most colleges have these programs, but some are more extensive than others. I know of no source that has evaluated them and listed the most outstanding. While *The College Handbook* of the College Entrance Examination Board is a good source for determining if a college has an honors program, further information would have to be obtained directly from each college.

COOPERATIVE EDUCATION

Many colleges and universities offer programs in which students attend college part of the year and work in private industry in jobs related to their majors the rest of the time. Frequently, these programs require a fifth year of college for an undergraduate degree.

The chief advantages of these programs are that the student earns money while he is working, so he is able to pay a high portion of the cost of his education, and that he generally has less difficulty in finding a job following graduation. Both of these are important considerations. Some schools claim, for instance, that if a student can afford the first two years of college, he can probably earn enough to finance the final three years.

I don't have to stress how important a consideration jobs are. Many students graduate from college today only to become cab drivers, secretaries, carpenters, etc., jobs that traditionally have not required college educations. It's common for women to graduate from four-year colleges and then attend secretarial school when they can't find jobs.

One of the chief assets a cooperative student can present when he applies for employment is his work experience. Since he's actually worked in private industry, he has more than the theory of the classroom to offer. He can obtain recommendations from employers as well as professors. And I'll bet that the employers carry more weight. Moreover, a high percentage of coop students begin work immediately for their coop employers following graduation. They're a known quantity. Somebody else is a stranger, no matter how outstanding his credentials.

Recently I read an article about an English major at Yale who had written to all the major newspapers on the East Coast and couldn't find employment anywhere. If a Yale student experienced this kind of response, what are the chances of the average student at the average college? If this student had majored in, say, petroleum engineering or computer science, I doubt that she would have a problem. Still, I can't help wondering whether she might not have been more successful had she been in a coop program.

A little while ago I chatted with an employer in the financial services field. His pessimistic view was that the "fat" days of the fifties, sixties, and early seventies are over. Companies are no longer willing to hire students, place them in management-training programs, and teach them from scratch. Some adjustment and training may still be necessary, of course, but nothing comparable to what once existed. He felt sorry for applicants who came in with liberal arts degrees. As he put it, "They're absolutely unemployable."

The chief disadvantage of coop programs is probably the effect upon a student's social life. Colleges with these programs tend to have less stable populations, since students are constantly coming and going as they begin or end their coop work.

All in all, the financial savings and, probably most crucial, the increased employment opportunities make this a very attractive choice. Many colleges and universities offer coop programs as an option, but relatively few students actually take advantage of them. Here is a list of schools that are heavily involved, although even with some of them, coop enrolls a minority of their students:

University of Akron
Antioch College
Auburn University
Beloit College
Bennington College
California State
  University at Fullerton
California State
  University at
  Dominguez Hills
University of Cincinnati
Cleveland State
  University

University of Detroit
Drexel University
Georgia Institute of
  Technology
Northeastern University
Rochester Institute of
  Technology
Texas A and M
  University
Virginia Polytechnic
  Institute and State
  University
Wilberforce University

The following two institutions could have been included in the previous list, since they have coop programs, but both are unusual enough to merit a brief description of their programs.

GMI Engineering and Management Institute

From 1919 until July 1, 1982, General Motors Institute, the West Point of the automotive industry, was the only accredited undergraduate college owned by a corporation. During these years General Motors Institute became famous for educating almost all of the top management of General Motors as well as a large part of the management of their competition in the automotive industry.

On July 1, 1982, however, a historic change took place. General Motors Institute became the GMI Engineering and Management Institute, an independent college; and as many as half of the students in the future will be sponsored by and work for corporations other than General Motors. New sponsors include U.S. Steel, Eastman Kodak, Cooper Tire, Rockwell International, TRW, Bendix, Eaton, and Gulf and Western. By the fall of 1983 the Institute expects to have more than two hundred companies as sponsors.

GMI Engineering and Management Institute will continue to offer three bachelors degrees in engineering (mechanical, industrial, and electrical) and one in industrial administration. A student must be accepted by the institute as well as sponsored by a company for which he will work during his times of employment. Freshmen average $6,500 a year in earnings with General Motors Corporation, and the earnings of students employed by other sponsors should be comparable. Tuition for 1982–83 is $1,800, and room and board is $1,650. A student's earnings for five years at the institute should easily cover all of his expenses.

The chief disadvantage of the institute is the social life. A student can't fool around when he's going to school for his employer. There are terrific advantages, on the other hand. The education and work experience can't be duplicated elsewhere. Rather than looking for jobs, the graduates would already be working for major corporations. Especially talented students may be able to continue their studies at company expense after graduation, a practice General Motors has followed. The cost of the institute is low, and the earnings are excellent.

If a student is capable and ambitious, this could eventually lead all the way to the top. That's why the institute was created.

THE COLLEGE OF INSURANCE

The College of Insurance (TCI) is the only baccalaureate degree–granting institution in the United States established by and supported by a particular industry. TCI offers a bachelor of business administration degree with a major in insurance or a bachelor of science degree with a major in actuarial science (this means learning to apply the laws of mathematical probability to the problems of business and commerce). The length of the program is five years. The school year is broken into four-month segments, with the students either taking courses or working for an insurance company during each segment. Each student is sponsored by an insurance company, for which he will work during his coop periods and by which two-thirds of his tuition and fees will be paid. He is also assured of earning at least $12,000 while he is in college, so his expenses should be pretty well covered.

TCI is located in downtown Manhattan, not far from Wall Street and Greenwich Village. Its campus is an office building, and students are housed at the St. George Hotel, in Brooklyn, and at Wagner College, on Staten Island. The Insurance Library of the college is the largest and most comprehensive in the world.

Like GMI Engineering and Management Institute, this is not the place for the student who wants to have a good time and the rah, rah college life. However, for the right student who wants a good education for almost nothing, a sure job upon graduation, a future in the insurance industry, and the experience of living in New York City, this is a terrific deal.

THE MILITARY OPTION

If a young man or woman is willing to serve in the military, there are outstanding opportunities available for saving money on educational expenses. Some are so tempting that it's surprising they aren't more eagerly pursued, although more students have started to take advantage of these options as jobs have become harder to find and college aid has decreased. In fact, the lure of aid toward college expenses is fast becoming the focus of much military advertising.

The image of the military as authoritarian and slightly dangerous to a young person's health reduces its appeal, and in truth it's hard to argue against these negative aspects. They're fundamental to any military force, although I suspect that these fears may be unduly exaggerated in some people's minds.

The armed forces can be helpful in regard to future employment. Everyone is aware of the training available to enlisted personnel, but less well known is the fact that many employers simply like to hire someone who has had military experience. Let's say that two people apply for a job, both of them holding degrees in business administration. If one of the two has been an officer in the service, he will have an advantage, because he has held a position of responsibility in a large organization and has experienced the difficulties involved in trying to accomplish something in such an organization. The other applicant can show only that he's been a successful student, and the qualities that lead to success in the classroom aren't necessarily those that lead to success in a company. Colleges even have a maxim that recognizes this fact: "Be kind to your average students. Your outstanding students will become professors, but someday your average students will endow the college."

The military may not be for everyone, but it is a unique way of life that a person must experience to understand. The post-Vietnam generation can't remember the time when nearly everyone served in the military and so may not realize how much that training has affected our national character. A stint in the service offers increased insight into current affairs and the vision behind national policies, as well as a new perspective on historical events. To some extent, people who have not served in the military have missed something in life, are alienated from one large aspect of our culture.

THE MILITARY ACADEMIES

This is an especially attractive option for a student, because not only are the academies 100 percent free (tuition, room and board, and medical and dental care are provided), but they pay salaries, too, currently $461.40 per month. The major catch is that after graduation the student must fulfill a five-year active-duty obligation.

To enter the U.S. Air Force Academy, the U.S. Military Academy, or the U.S. Naval Academy, an applicant must first obtain a nomination, usually from his senator or congressman, although the president; the vice-president; the governors of Puerto Rico, the Canal Zone, and American Samoa; the delegates from Guam and the Virgin Islands; the delegate from the District of Columbia; and the resident commissioner of Puerto Rico all have one or more nominations (the president makes one hundred nominations a year). Active-duty personnel have even more possibilities.

Nominations are not easy to come by. Here's a recent profile of an entering class of the Naval Academy:

No. of candidates	7,100
Qualified scholastically, medically, physically	2,250
Offers of admission	1,708
Admitted	1,363

SAT Scores:	Verbal	Math
700—800	5%	35%
600—699	31%	52%
500—599	50%	12%
400—499	14%	1%
Mean Scores	570	664

ACT Scores:	English	Math
30—36	4%	54%
25—29	41%	45%
20—24	52%	1%
15—19	3%	0%
Mean Scores	24	31

School Honors and Activities

Student-body president or vice president	8%
Class president or vice president	9%
School-club president or vice president	23%
School-publication staff	28%
National Honor Society	47%
Varsity athletics	74%
Varsity letter winners	68%
Dramatics, public speaking, debating	52%
Leader of musical group	6%
Eagle Scout	9%
Boys'/Girls' State or Nation	14%
ROTC, NROTC, AFROTC	7%
Sea Cadets	2%

Rank in High-School Class

First fifth	79%
Second fifth	16%
Third fifth	4%
Fourth fifth	1%

My experience has been that the academies want a special kind of individual: one who not only is strong both academically and physically but has the ability to relate well to others and the capacity to lead them. Such students frequently demonstrate these abilities in high school through extracurricular sports and other activities such as clubs or publications. Brilliant but introverted loners may not be successful in their bids for the academies.

One key factor complicating an applicant's chances is the nomination process itself. There's an element of luck involved. For instance, a congressman is allowed five students at a time attending each academy. One year he may be able to nominate two, since one of his nominees may be graduating and another may have dropped out, but the following year he may not be able to nominate anyone if all five of his nominees still remain at the academy.

Also, an applicant is competing for a specific nomination, and this could vary in difficulty from place to place. For instance, a senator from Florida may have several very strong applicants, but a senator from Oklahoma may have only mediocre ones. If some of those outstanding prospects from Florida lived in Oklahoma, they'd have much better chances for appointments. Applying from Florida at that particular time, though, they could well lose out unless they're picked up by the president or vice-president. Conversely, an Oklahoma applicant might sneak in even though he'd have no chance if he had to compete against all of the applicants.

An applicant to any of these academies should begin the process in the spring of his junior year in high school. Detailed information may be obtained from: Director of Admissions and Registrar, U.S. Air Force Academy, U.S.A.F. Academy, Colorado 80840; Director of Admissions, U.S. Military Academy, West Point, New York 10996; or Director, Candidate Guidance, U.S. Naval Academy, Annapolis, Maryland 21402.

The U.S. Merchant Marine Academy is very similar to the first three described, in that a nomination is required for admittance, students live a military life, and all costs are borne by the U.S. government. On the other hand, there are substantial differences. All of its students remain civilians, even though uniforms are worn and the trappings of military discipline are observed. Also, entering plebes deposit $290 to cover the cost of uniforms, and they receive no pay while they are at the academy, except when they serve aboard ship. Midshipmen graduate with a B.S. degree, a license as a ship's officer, and a commission in the U.S. Naval Reserve. Ninety-two percent pursue careers in business and industry.

As with the other academies, application should commence in the spring of the junior year. Additional information may be obtained from: Admissions Office, U.S. Merchant Marine Academy, Kings Point, New York 11024.

There's still another academy, the U.S. Coast Guard Academy. Basically, it operates as the first three described, with one significant difference. Students apply to the Coast Guard Academy just as they would to any other college. No nomination is necessary. Since early application isn't as important, an applicant should probably plan to apply in the fall of his senior year. December 15 is the closing date for applications, but students should check to be sure that the date hasn't changed.

Currently, the futures of the Coast Guard and Coast Guard Academy are under a cloud. Their budgets have been cut, and there appear to be philosophical differences among the Coast Guard, the Department of Transportation, and the Office of Management and Budget. Some Coast Guard critics feel that its role has changed and that it serves little purpose as a military force. Whether the Coast Guard will continue to function in its present capacity is uncertain. Interested students should investigate before they apply.

Information can be obtained from: Director of Admissions, U.S. Coast Guard Academy, New London, Connecticut 06320.

An applicant who is rejected by an Academy need not radically change his life plan. College ROTC programs are one excellent substitute, but those who insist on an academy or nothing can join that branch of the service and try from within. A few years ago I counseled an outstanding young man. In spite of what I felt were his excellent credentials and his ideal attitude for the military, he failed to obtain a nomination to the U.S. Naval Academy. Consequently, he enlisted in the Navy and took a battery of tests, and the results sent his recruiters into ecstasy. His first assignment was to the Nuclear Power Program, which, I understand, is something of an honor. The next time I heard from him he was attending the Naval Academy Prep School at Newport, Rhode Island, and he continued on to the naval academy. In high school, most people thought he was a little crazy for wanting to join the Navy rather than start college, but his success proved them wrong.

ROTC PROGRAMS

There are two basic programs in the Reserve Officers Training Corps. First, a student can attend a college that has an ROTC unit and simply join the unit. During his junior and senior years he receives $100 a month, free uniforms, and ROTC textbooks. Upon graduation he is commissioned as an officer and has to serve on active duty for three years.

A second program is the scholarship program, which is much more selective. Under this program the military pays tuition, the cost of textbooks, any instructional fees, and a subsistence allowance of $100 a month for maximums of forty, thirty, and twenty months for four-year, three-year, and two-year programs. Graduates of these programs have a four-year active-duty obligation.

While most students are aware of the four-year scholarship program, the two- and three-year programs are additional possibilities. Freshmen in college can apply for the three-year scholarship, sophomores for the two-year. These two- and three-year scholarships are available to all students, although those in ROTC probably have a slight edge in the competition.

Speaking of competition, I can assure you that it is quite intense for the scholarship program, if my experience is representative of what is happening nationally. I've seen students with excellent academic credentials who were unsuccessful in their applications.

In addition, applicants must pass stringent physical examinations. Here are a few of the requirements for NROTC (Navy ROTC):

Height for Men. Navy, 62 to 78 inches; Marines, 66 to 78 inches.

Height for Women. Navy, 60 to 78 inches; Marines, 60 to 78 inches.

Weight. Proportional to height.

Eyes. Each eye 20/20 without correction. Limited waivers available for those whose vision corrects to 20/20 in both eyes where refractive error in each eye does not exceed ±5.50 diopters. Both eyes must be free of any disfiguring or incapacitating abnormality and from acute or chronic disease. Normal color vision is required for Navy ROTC candidates. Marine Corps–option candidates may be granted waivers for defective color vision.

Allergies. No hay fever or chronic rhinitis. No history of asthma since twelfth birthday.

Heart. Normal heartbeat. No hypertension or history of cardiovascular ailment.

Joints. No internal derangement or residuals of serious injury.

Teeth. Excellent dental health. Minimum of eight serviceable teeth each arch.

One NROTC applicant I know had spots on his teeth that looked as though they might be the start of decay. He couldn't pass his physical until he had those spots filled, even though his dentist swore that they were not the start of decay and didn't require filling. After he had them filled, he wasn't selected for the scholarship program anyway.

These scholarship programs are in demand, and the military can be very selective. And they should be. They're laying out a lot of money. At some expensive colleges the four-year program is costing the government well over $30,000 per recipient.

Most high-school guidance offices have bulletins from the various ROTC branches, so they are probably the easiest places for high-school students to gain more detailed information. A potential applicant must first analyze which colleges offer ROTC and which branches they offer. If the local high school lacks this kind of information, literature can be obtained directly from the following addresses: Air Force ROTC, Maxwell AFB, Alabama 36112; Army ROTC, Fort Monroe, Virginia 23651; Commandant of the Marine Corps, (Code MRRO-6), Headquarters, U.S. Marine Corps, Washington, D.C. 20380; Commander, Navy Recruiting Command, (Code 314), 4015 Wilson Boulevard, Arlington, Virginia 22203.

A final note concerning these programs. The application process begins well before an applicant would apply to college. Normally, application can begin as early as March of an applicant's junior year in high school, and the deadline is December 1 of the senior year. (Applicants should double-check these dates, since they may vary from year to year and branch to branch.) Moreover, applicants who file early have a better chance of acceptance since there is both an early selection board and a final selection. Essentially, an early applicant has two chances for acceptance and a late applicant only one.

ENLISTMENT IN THE MILITARY

There are so many potential opportunities here that it's hard to know where to begin. For the sake of brevity this discussion will concentrate on the Navy, but as a practical matter the other services have similar programs. Sometimes they change the names, but the basic benefits are there. Here are the programs:

Navy Campus. This is a program in which civilian educational specialists help Navy personnel reach their educational objectives. There are many aspects: counseling to assure realistic goals, help in obtaining credit for civilian and Navy education toward high school and college degrees, assistance in finding appropriate formal education, and help in obtaining financial assistance from Navy and other funding sources.

In addition, there are eighteen two- and four-year colleges affiliated with the Navy through what is known as the Certificate/Degree Program. These colleges waive residency requirements, which means that Navy personnel can receive a degree without ever attending a single class. They must meet the college's graduation requirement, however.

Students who enroll in one of these colleges sign a letter of agreement that specifies the course of study they must follow in order to receive a degree or certificate, and they have ten years to complete the program. Credit is awarded both for credits successfully pursued at other institutions and for nontraditional education. All of these colleges allow at least 75 percent of the credits and some as much as 80 percent in nontraditional education. Here are examples of nontraditional education:

1. ACE recommendation for Navy training course completion. (The American Council on Education or ACE evaluates Navy courses and recommends the amount of credit that should be awarded for completion of the courses. ACE also translates Navy courses taken at Navy technical schools into course titles at civilian institutions.)
2. ACE recommendation for Navy ratings (work experience)
3. On-the-job training

4. Accredited independent-study courses
5. Proficiency/Challenge examinations
6. Experiential learning
7. CLEP general exam and subject exams
8. ACT proficiency exam
9. DANTES subject standardized tests (DANTES, Defense Activity for Non-Traditional Education Support, is a Department of Defense agency that delivers and documents for accreditation educational experiences that do not take place in a formal classroom.)
10. College Board Advanced Placement tests
11. Graduate Record Examination (GRE) advanced tests
12. Transcript courses from other service schools

In addition to the Certificate/Degree Program, the Navy also has SOC (Servicemen's Opportunity College), in which several hundred two- and four-year colleges and universities participate. The fundamental purpose of this program is to establish a home base to which the student can have his credits sent from the various colleges he attends as he is shipped around the country and the world. While many of these colleges are also liberal in awarding nontraditional credit to students, generally they're not quite as flexible as those involved in the Certificate/Degree Program.

PACE (Program for Afloat College Education). The Navy sponsors tuition-free college courses for crew members serving on ships at sea. Most of the courses are at the freshman or sophomore level, and all are offered by accredited institutions of higher education.

BOOST (Broadened Opportunity for Officer Selection and Training). Ambitious young men and women who are not adequately prepared to compete on an equal basis with other students applying for NROTC scholarships or the Naval Academy receive another opportunity through BOOST. Those admitted to this program attend BOOST School in San Diego, California, for eleven months of college-preparatory training. Those selected for the academy or for NROTC scholarships (92 percent of a recent class qualified for one or the other) receive an additional six to eight weeks of orientation.

EEAP (Enlisted Education Advancement Program). This program offers active-duty personnel the opportunity to attend junior or community colleges full-time and earn associate in arts or science degrees in twenty-four months.

ECP (The Enlisted Commissioning Program). This program enables outstanding active-duty personnel with previous college credits to complete baccalaureate degrees in twenty-four months through full-time study at NROTC colleges or universities.

Navy Tuition Assistance versus VEAP (Veterans Educational Assistance Program). The Navy pays up to 75 percent of tuition for active-duty personnel at civilian educational institutions. Compare this with VEAP, a program that offers two dollars of government money for every dollar contributed by a serviceman toward his education. Currently, in the Navy, $8,100 can be accumulated in this manner, but the VEAP program varies from year to year and from branch to branch. For example, when I investigated this, the Navy representative was unhappy with the present situation, noting that it had been much better last year and might improve again in the next fiscal year. She explained that the attractiveness of VEAP varies with the need for enlistments and the congressional appropriation.

The Army offers the following for a two-year enlistment:

$100   per month contributed by
serviceman
× 24   months

$2,400
+ $4,800   government 2 for 1

$7,200
+ $8,000   Army College Fund Bonus

$15,200   total toward college expenses

Who knows? Maybe next year the Navy will have the better VEAP. Those who are interested should compare when they enlist.

THE MILITARY AND A BACHELOR'S DEGREE

To demonstrate how economically and expeditiously one can obtain a degree with Navy assistance, let me illustrate with an example from Navy literature. Tom Nagle, Jr., graduated from the University of Maryland with a bachelor's degree in business management. He obtained his credits in the following manner:

Navy Schools	21 credits
Navy Ratings	21 credits
CLEP Tests	24 credits
DANTES Tests	6 credits
Univ. of Maryland	51 credits

He earned seventy-two semester hours of credit (more than half the credits needed for a bachelor's degree) without spending any money of his own or even attending the university. He received his degree after only fifteen months spent in formal classes.

FOREIGN STUDY

An idea that might be suitable for an unusual student is to attend college in another country. In most nations higher education is fundamentally financed by the government, so American tuitions usually look sky-high in comparison. In addition to the inexpensive education offered, an American student can gain exposure to another culture and possibly another language.

On the other hand, the educational systems of many nations differ drastically from ours. Most make no attempt to educate as large a proportion of their population as we do, but those they concentrate on are exposed to extremely rigorous curriculums; courses such as chemistry and physics in eighth and ninth grade, for instance, are not unusual. The April 12, 1982, issue of *U.S. News and World Report* had an article that illustrated these differences. It showed that for every thousand people, the United States has fifty-two college students, France twenty-one, Italy nineteen, Belgium eighteen, West Germany seventeen, and Britain thirteen. Closer to home, Canada has thirty-six and Mexico ten.

Canada probably offers the most easily obtainable foreign education. There are many universities, and the language of instruction is English at all of the main universities except Laval, Montreal, and Sherbrooke, where it is French. The University of Ottawa has instruction in both languages. Many Americans are accepted by Canadian universities each year, so this doesn't appear to be a problem, although some provinces require thirteen years of school prior to the university. Tuitions have been for the most part quite reasonable, about $1,500 to $2,000 a year, although they vary considerably from university to university. McGill University recently increased tuition to the point where it's no longer a bargain.

Canadian higher education differs in certain respects from American. A bachelor's degree takes from three to five years. A student may study for either a general (pass) bachelor's degree or for an honors bachelor's degree. The honors degree program normally involves an additional year of study, is open only to those with high academic standing, and requires a greater concentration in one or two subjects. Students who wish to continue their educations toward an advanced degree at a Canadian university should have completed an honors bachelor's degree. Further information can be obtained from AUCC Information, 1S1 Slater, Ottawa, Canada, K1P 5N1.

Mexico might present more of a problem to most students since the instruction is normally in Spanish. If one is fortunate enough to be fluent in Spanish, an excellent possibility is the University of Mexico in Mexico City. This is a huge university with approximately 74,000 full-time and part-time students, located on a fifteen-hundred-acre, attractive, modern campus. Tuition is nominal; recently it was $160 a year. Mexico City is beautiful and cosmopolitan, and it has a year-round springlike climate. Many people feel that it's the perfect place to go to college. For information, write to Universidad Nacional Autónoma de México, Departamento de Información al Extranjero, Torre de la Rectoria, Cuidad Universitaria, México 20, D.F.

A non–Spanish speaking student might consider the University of the Americas, where many of the courses are offered in English. This essentially American-style institution, fully accredited by the Southern Association of Schools and Colleges (one of the main accrediting bodies in the U.S.), is located in Puebla, a city of 750,000. It lies about eighty miles east of Mexico City. Current tuition and fees are about $750, and a double room is about $150 a year. Campus meals are roughly $5 a day. For information, write to Universidad de las Américas, Apdo. Postal 100, Sta. Catarina Martir, Puebla, México.

Although it's not a foreign nation, Puerto Rico offers the non–Spanish speaking American the same advantages and disadvantages as Mexico. Tuitions are low, although the public colleges and universities charge non–Puerto Ricans higher rates. One major advantage of Puerto Rico is that Americans can apply for federal financial aid just as they would anywhere else in the United States. Another is that they are accredited by United States accrediting agencies, so transferring credit to another American college is relatively simple.

The Catholic University of Puerto Rico is one possibility for someone who isn't fluent in Spanish. While the majority of its courses are offered in Spanish, it is a bilingual university, and a student could study in English until he felt competent in Spanish. Otherwise, it's a thoroughly American university. It even requires the SAT. Tuition is $40 a credit, a dormitory room (semiprivate for women and private for men) is $200 a semester, and meals are $200 a semester. Interested students should write to Office of Admissions, Catholic University of Puerto Rico, Ponce, Puerto Rico 00731.

Some students may be interested in the Hebrew University of Jerusalem, which opened in 1925 and returned to its original Mount Scorpus campus in 1967 after the reunification of Jerusalem. American students who lack an adequate knowledge of Hebrew spend the first year in the Rothberg School for Overseas Students preparing for regular study at the university, then obtain their B.A. or B.S. degrees in three more years. Yearly tuition for 1982–83 is $1,600. For information, write to Office of Academic Affairs, American Friends of Hebrew University, 1140 Avenue of the Amcricas, New York, New York 10036.

European universities look attractive to many Americans who would enjoy living in Europe, and European tuitions are usually cheap. In West Germany, for instance, tuition is free; and in Italy and Spain it's only about $100 or $200 a year. England has become more expensive recently, however.

Unfortunately, it's not easy for an American to take advantage of European universities. In the first place, there could be a language problem. Second, admissions standards are quite high, and even natives of these countries frequently have difficulty gaining entrance to a university. Third, students face more arduous preparation than the typical American college-prep students. Since most European nations feel that their own students are two years ahead of American students, they won't even consider an American applicant unless he has already completed a couple of years of college.

The distinction between American and European educations stems from a basic difference in educational philosophies and in methods of financing higher education. The European philosophy is elitist. Only the very best are admitted, after years of grueling preparation. In some places, such as England, this intellectual elitism is also reflected in the class structure. Since European universities are public and heavily subsidized by the governments, there is a financial incentive as well as a philosophical reason for keeping the numbers of students relatively low.

The United States, on the other hand, is more egalitarian. Since we like to think of everyone as equal, we consider everyone a logical candidate for college. This is the land of the late bloomer. While some American institutions are quite selective, many others will accept absolutely any high school graduate, and frequently they'll waive even that requirement. Unlike Europe, the United States also has both private and public institutions, which compete intensely for students, so much so that the major task of many college administrators is dreaming up ways to attract more applicants.

Given the vast difference between American and European educations, most American students who study in Europe do so under the auspices of an American college or university, as part of a junior year abroad, for instance. Still, quite a few Americans are studying in Europe and working toward European degrees. It's possible, but it's not easy.

Although it's not inexpensive, one European university that is willing to accept American students directly from high school is the University of St. Andrews in Scotland. According to an article in the *Chronicle of Higher Education*, St. Andrews has begun to recruit American students because, with declining government support and attendant increased tuition, the numbers of foreign students have been falling. Since the Scottish system of education is closer to the American than the English, St. Andrews feels that American students who are well prepared for college should be able to fit in. Students with SATs of 1200 or better should be at least as capable as Scottish university students. If St. Andrews is successful in its efforts, other universities in Great Britain could become more accessible to Americans.

Described by one observer as a Scottish Oxford, St.

Andrews was founded in 1411, making it one of the oldest universities in Great Britain. It is located fifty miles north of Edinburgh on the coast of Fife in a small seaside town of the same name, near some of the most famous golf courses in Scotland. St. Andrews has two colleges: St. Mary's for the study of divinity, and the United College of St. Salvator and St. Leonard for the arts, science, and medical fields. Tuition at St. Andrews is $5,000 a year except for a science major, which costs $7,000. Housing averages about $1,800 a year. Interested students should write to the Office of the Dean (at the appropriate college), St. Andrews KY 16 9AJ, Scotland.

This discussion of foreign educational opportunities barely scratches the surface. Students who wish to explore this subject in detail can find much useful information in *The New Guide To Study Abroad*, 1981–82, by John A. Garraty, Lily von Klemperer, and Cyril J. H. Taylor (New York: Harper and Row); and in the *Whole World Handbook*, by Marjorie Adoff Cohen (New York: E. P. Dutton), 1981–82 edition.

9

NO-NEED SCHOLARSHIPS

Designed to attract very capable academic students or unusual students who can help the college in some way (athletically or musically, perhaps), these scholarships are granted without regard to the family's ability to pay. A Rockefeller could qualify for one of these. Especially valuable since they continue from year to year provided the recipient maintains an acceptable academic record, these awards have been growing in popularity. Even so, they are still relatively rare, and many colleges offer none. Appendix 1 lists many of the available awards, ranging from continuing financial support to smaller, one-time prizes.

Ironically, these awards are expanding at the same time that money devoted to need-based aid is contracting, seemingly because more and more colleges are experiencing difficulty attracting the kind of student that they would really like to have. Some college officials deplore this no-need trend and refer deprecatingly to them as "enticement" scholarships. They maintain that no-need awards take money away from need-based aid, and that institutions using these awards are "enticing" students to their campuses. Whether one agrees with them or not, the critics appear to be waging a losing battle.

ACADEMIC SCHOLARSHIPS

The category that is growing most rapidly involves purely academic or talent (music or art) scholarships. These scholarships are ideal for families concerned about costs, especially at private colleges. As a matter of fact, that's one of the main reasons so many private colleges have begun to establish them. When a private school offers a partial scholarship to a highly capable student, it neutralizes the price advantage of a public college and becomes able to compete successfully for the students it wants. Quite a few state schools also offer them now, though, so the battle for talent is heating up.

Institutions that offer these awards tend to talk in lofty terms about their desire to reward scholarship. They give them titles such as the President's Scholarship or Alumni Merit Awards. While honoring scholarship may indeed be one of their purposes, I doubt that it's the only one. There's a strong element of self-interest, too.

Most of these schools are buying brains, talent, and leadership for their student body. When a school adds forty or fifty students whose credentials are substantially better than those of the students who typically attend, a lot of things are changed. The average SAT or ACT scores, which are published, look better. The number of National Merit semifinalists, also published, increases. Those forty or fifty students tend to become leaders in various activities—editors of the yearbook or newspaper, for instance. They help the college to compare favorably to other schools in areas such as debates and musical programs. They add luster to the college by capturing academic honors such as Rhodes Scholarships. Finally, they add intellectual vigor to the campus, which makes everybody happy, most of all probably the professors.

From this we derive a basic rule for anyone who wants an academic scholarship: Find a college that is less impressive than you would normally think of attending. You have to drop down a notch or two. For instance, if a student has an SAT score of 1150, a college with average scores of 1100 isn't very likely to wildly toss money in his direction and break out the champagne, unless he has a lot more going for him than his scores. A college with average boards in the 900s might feel different.

Our rule implies that the most competitive colleges in the nation don't have to offer no-need scholarships, since they already have their pick of the best candidates, and that is basically the way it is. Most don't offer any; if they do, they're inconsequential. For instance, Dartmouth offers a Daniel Webster Scholarship based purely on talent, but it's for only $150 a year. Considering the total costs at Dartmouth, this scholarship is merely honorary. A few very prestigious schools offer no-need scholarships (Duke, Swarthmore, Johns Hopkins, Emory, Vanderbilt, and Rice, for instance), but they are a distinct minority.

One of the most surprising things I've ever encountered as a counselor has been the indifference that most capable students show toward no-need scholarships. When I first started to publicize them in the high school in which I work, I expected to be inundated by students eagerly pursuing them. Instead, almost nothing happened. Except for a handful of adventurous souls, most students have remained completely oblivious. Our counseling staff has even tried talking students into applying—and has usually failed.

Upon reflection, I have arrived at two theories. First, many families apparently feel guilty not sending a child who has been an outstanding student to the college of his first choice, even if it is quite expensive. After all, we're talking about a terrific kid, the apple of their eye. After he's worked so hard at his studies, isn't not sending him tantamount to refusing to pay him after he's cut the grass? Second, other families who anticipate qualifying for financial aid have grown confident that their aid will largely obviate the need for a merit scholarship. Why accept a second-choice school when the financial difference is probably insignificant?

I have already discussed the ramifications of spending much more than is necessary for an education, so I won't belabor the point. As for families that are counting on aid, they would be wise to remember that financial aid may not be as plentiful as before, at least in the immediate future. More will be expected of both parents and students, and large loans will become the norm. Under these circumstances, ignoring merit awards could be very expensive.

ATHLETIC SCHOLARSHIPS

Any high-school athlete who possesses talent, not necessarily exceptional, in one or more sports may be eligible for either an athletic scholarship or at least more favorable consideration for financial aid. Briefly, this is the situation:

Men's sports are administered by the NCAA (the National Collegiate Athletic Association). The NCAA has established three divisions for member institutions, based on the size of the college and the caliber of athletic competition it faces. Considerable overlapping can occur, however, since colleges may compete in different divisions in different sports. For instance, a college that is normally Division II might have a Division III wrestling team and a Division I hockey team.

In men's sports, athletic scholarships are limited to Division I and II teams, and even these divisions are limited in how many scholarships they can offer. Division III can offer only financial aid based upon need.

Major recruitment of athletes is normally confined to Division I. The frantic recruitment that is sometimes seen involves football and basketball, the revenue-producing sports. Institutions with top football and basketball teams frequently finance their entire athletic programs with the receipts from these two sports. Athletes talented enough to compete in these sports on the Division I level don't pursue scholarships. Scholarships pursue them.

In the last decade women's sports have been administered by the AIAW (the Association for Intercollegiate Athletics for Women), but it appears that the AIAW may be collapsing and its members rejoining the NCAA.

In any case, women's sports will probably approximate men's. For instance, the AIAW has three divisions. Division I can offer up to 100 percent of permissible athletic aid, Division II up to 50 percent, and Division III up to 10 percent. If schools rejoin the NCAA, these totals could change a bit, but Division I is still going to be able to do more than Division III.

Increased emphasis has been placed on women's sports recently by the enactment of Title IX, which forces institutions to equalize their efforts between men's and women's athletics. Consequently, some larger institutions that formerly concentrated on men's sports have begun upgrading women's sports. A representative of a small college that has had good women's athletics through the years recently observed that some of these larger institutions are now in the process of building powerhouses in women's sports, and he questions whether his institution will be able to compete successfully in the future. Last year one of his top female athletic prospects laughed when she heard how much aid his institution could offer. A large state university had already offered her twice as much.

Another aspect of athletic scholarships is that even though a team may be allowed to offer athletic scholarships according to NCAA or AIAW rules, it may be prevented from offering them by the philosophy of the school or the rules of its league. The Ivy League, for instance, doesn't offer athletic scholarships, although their admissions officers undoubtedly do their utmost to prove that a highly desirable athlete has substantial need. (One observer feels that Ivy League schools have trouble competing in popular men's sports such as football because of the absence of scholarships and the scarcity of football players who are talented both athletically and academically. However, they don't have as much trouble attracting female students with these qualities, and some of their women's teams are strong.)

Financial aid is also a major factor in athletics. Division I schools in track, for instance, are limited to eleven scholarships, but they need much larger teams to remain competitive. Consequently, sometimes they make highly attractive offers to athletes based purely on financial need, and then those athletes don't count against their scholarship limits. Also, especially in football, sometimes an institution brings a player to campus on financial aid and has him work out with the team but not play. Such an athlete may be ineligible to enter as a freshman because of his high-school grades, or perhaps his value to the team is not certain. If things work out, they can offer him a scholarship for the following year, and then he still has four years of eligibility left.

Another aspect of financial aid and athletics is that athletes who qualify for state and federal money on the basis of need don't cost the institutions as much as athletes who fail to qualify. If a school's athletic scholarship is worth $6,000 a year, for instance, an athlete who qualifies for $4,000 in federal and state aid would cost the college only $2,000. Recently the University of Oklahoma calculated that forty male and female athletes received $30,000 in Pell grants. The university didn't state how much those forty may have also received in SEOG or state grants, or other scholarships, nor whether they were the only forty athletes who qualified for nonuniversity money. Ironically, needy athletes are more desirable than affluent ones from an institutional viewpoint.

To summarize, there are many advantages available to students with athletic talent. It is easier for them to gain admission to a college, which is especially helpful at the highly competitive institutions. If a student athlete qualifies for need-based aid rather than scholarships, his aid package is likely to be more attractive than the packages offered other students: high grant and/or appealing campus job and low loan, for instance. Lastly, he may obtain an actual athletic scholarship.

Except for the recruitment of athletes for major sports at Division I institutions, most recruitment is pretty haphazard. Sometimes a college coach hears about a high-school player from one of his friends or former players, or one of the alumni writes about a good prospect for his alma mater. Frequently it's possible for an athlete to bring himself to a coach's attention.

If a student wishes to try for an athletic scholarship or other aid, he should first investigate which institutions field teams on the level at which he can compete, and then he should narrow his possibilities according to other factors such as curriculum or location. Second, he should write to the coaches of the teams he'd like to play for, briefly describing himself and his accomplishments (both athletic and academic) and expressing his desire to attend their institutions and play for their teams.

High-school coaches are frequently able to offer advice to their players concerning appropriate colleges. In addition, many high-school guidance offices have copies of the *Directory of College Athletics,* a yearly publication that has both a men's and a women's edition. These books list the colleges, their conferences, the names of their coaches, and their addresses and phone numbers. Copies may be obtained from Ray Franks Publishing, P.O. Box 7068, Amarillo, Texas 79109 ($12 for the men's edition, $8 for the women's).

There's a world of opportunity out there for good athletes who are smart enough to realize that most college coaches won't automatically beat a path to their doors.

10

COLLEGE CREDIT BY EXAMINATION

Talented students who test well may find that they can save money, time, and effort by taking examinations for college credit. The two main routes are either AP (Advanced Placement) or CLEP (College-Level Examination Program). Both of these are offered by the College Board. In addition, there is PEP (Proficiency Examination Program) of American College Testing, but these tests are normally administered as a part of programs offered by organizations such as the military services or the Regents External-Degree Program of New York State.

ADVANCED PLACEMENT

Advanced Placement credits are accepted almost everywhere, by even the most competitive colleges. Normally, to take an AP test an applicant should first have taken an AP course, since these courses are specifically designed to prepare students for AP exams. However, if a student studies an AP Course Description and does the work and reading necessary to get a passing grade, he can also receive credit. Since these exams are so demanding, relatively few students are logical candidates for the courses, much less the exams. High schools that offer AP courses usually reserve them for the cream of their student body.

An applicant for AP exams must register through his high school or, if his school doesn't offer the exams or the applicant doesn't attend school, through a neighboring school. The exams are normally administered in late May (May 17–21 in 1982), but high schools typically enroll students in February and March so that they can order the right number of exams. Almost all of the exams are three hours each in length.

AP exams are offered in the following areas:

Art
History of Art
Studio Art: Drawing or
 General Portfolio

Biology

Chemistry

English
Language and
 Composition
Composition and
 Literature

French
Language (Level 3)
Literature (Level 3)

German
Language (Level 3)
Literature (Level 3)

History
American
European

Latin
Vergil
Catullus to Horace

Mathematics
Calculus (AB)
Calculus (BC)

Music
Listening and Literature
Theory

Physics (B)

Physics (C)
Mechanics
Electricity and
 Magnetism

Spanish
Language (Level 3)
Literature (Level 3)

CLEP

CLEP is accepted by more than eighteen hundred U.S. colleges and universities, but not by some of the very competitive ones. CLEP adheres to the philosophy that knowledge can be gained anywhere, and that if a testee who has never taken a course can score as high as the average person who has taken the course, the testee should receive college credit based on his knowledge. CLEP has been used by many mature people who have been out of school for some time, as well as by many recent high-school graduates. Unlike AP, there are no set curricula to be used in preparing for the exams.

CLEP offers five General Examinations in English Composition, Humanities, Mathematics, Natural Sciences, and Social Sciences and History. Considered introductory exams, they are used by colleges to determine credit. In addition, though, there are forty-seven Subject Exams in the following areas:

Business
Computers and Data
  Processing
Elementary Computer
  Programming:
  FORTRAN IV
Introduction to
  Management
Introductory Accounting
Introductory Business
  Law
Introductory Marketing

Composition and
  Literature
American Literature
Analysis and
  Interpretation of
  Literature
College Composition
English Literature
Freshman English

*Social Sciences and
  History*
Afro-American History
American Government
American History I:
  Early Colonizations to
  1877
American History II:
  1865 to the Present
Educational Psychology
General Psychology
Human Growth and
  Development
Introductory
  Macroeconomics
Introductory
  Microeconomics
Introductory Micro- and
  Macroeconomics
Introductory Sociology
Money and Banking
Western Civilization I:
  Ancient Near East to
  1648

*Dental Auxiliary
  Education*
Dental Materials
Head, Neck, and Oral
  Anatomy
Oral Radiography
Tooth Morphology and
  Function

Foreign Languages
College French (Levels 1
  and 2)
College German (Levels
  1 and 2)
College Spanish (Levels
  1 and 2)

Science and Mathematics
Calculus with
  Elementary Functions
College Algebra
College Algebra and
  Trigonometry
General Biology
General Chemistry
Statistics

Nursing
Anatomy, Physiology,
  Microbiology
Behavioral Sciences for
  Nurses
Fundamentals of
  Nursing
Medical-Surgical
  Nursing

Medical Technology
Clinical Chemistry
Hematology
Immunohematology and
  Blood Banking
Microbiology

There are two major advantages for students who are able to gain college credits through examination. First, there is a considerable financial saving. An AP exam costs $42, and CLEP exams cost $22 for the first and $18 for each additional exam taken on the same date. (AP is more expensive because each exam has a subjective portion that must be graded. Most CLEP exams are purely objective; if there is a required or optional subjective portion, it is sent to receiving colleges for grading.) Both AP and CLEP exams cost far less than the college courses they represent. Second, a student can move immediately into more advanced work rather than wasting time in a course that he basically understands. For instance, instead of starting with the introductory course in English Composition that most freshmen take, a student could begin with an English elective.

A possible disadvantage is that unless a student is ready for more advanced work, he may face a difficult transition when he finds himself competing against sophomores and juniors from the very start of his college career. In general, though, most students who have taken these exams and won the right to go on to more advanced work are pleased.

Students who wish to pursue CLEP credits should understand that they are not universally accepted. For instance, one small liberal-arts college that prides itself on the high acceptance rate of its graduates into graduate school has mixed feelings about CLEP. Some faculty members feel that they should accept CLEP credits, while others fear that this might mean a lowering of standards, which would be disastrous if the graduate schools then started to view their graduates less favorably. Consequently, this college doesn't accept CLEP unless the student is able to also pass departmental exams for the credits he earned through CLEP. For example, the college picks up a few students each year from community colleges that accept CLEP. When these students transfer, however, they find that their CLEP credits from community college are not accepted unless they can pass departmental exams. However, if an older pupil who had worked for a few years wanted to transfer credits, and he wasn't pre-med or pre-dent, the college might be more receptive.

Despite these potential problems, many students have benefited from CLEP. An article in the Philadelphia *Evening Bulletin* described a twenty-year-old student, Sandy Stanaitis, who took CLEP tests while she was enrolled at Widener. Up to that point she had earned sixty-two credits through CLEP, about half of what she needed to graduate.

Interested in more subjects than she could carry on her regular academic agenda, Miss Stanaitis learned about the program in her freshman year and started it in the second semester in 1977.

The testing intrigued her at first, and then the more tests she took the more of a "game" it became, "because it was so much fun to be learning on my own," she says.

She bought textbooks in the outside courses and could manage them because, "I love to read at night; I love to read all the time." Does it take a great deal of self-discipline? "Not so much," she answers. "I guess I'm just a studier." And certainly she is a self-motivator.

For tackling the first batch of tests, she drew mainly on "what I had in my head," some of which she had learned at Nether Providence High School.

CLEP exams are administered during the third week of each month except February and December, at a wide variety of colleges and universities. Anyone seeking more detailed literature should write to The College Board, Box 1822, Princeton, New Jersey 08541.

Some of the colleges and universities that accept CLEP credits are Auburn University, University of Southern California, Colorado School of Mines, George Washington University, Emory University, DePaul University, Tulane University, University of Maryland, University of Massachusetts, Michigan State University, Fairleigh Dickinson University, Hobart and William Smith Colleges, Penn State University, Texas Christian University, and Beloit College.

Some of the colleges and universities that do not normally accept CLEP credit are all of the Ivy League schools, Massachusetts Institute of Technology, Amherst College, Bryn Mawr College, Rice University, Stanford University, California Institute of Technology, Duke University, Georgetown University, Oberlin College, Middlebury College, and Wesleyan University.

Remember that the policies of institutions that accept AP, CLEP, or both differ widely. Some will accept sixty credits or more toward a degree, while others are more stringent. Some will use an exam merely for placement, allowing a student to skip a course but not giving him credit toward a degree from that course. Some will accept only the Subject Exams, not the General Exams, of CLEP. Students should investigate the colleges they're interested in.

Philosophically, educators are divided over the merit of CLEP. Although AP exams are generally accepted because they are so demanding and cover a structured body of knowledge, CLEP is more controversial. A colleague of mine, for instance, holds that talented youngsters who utilize CLEP are cheating themselves. He argues that a wide range of students reach U.S. colleges, and that the gifted ones should seek out those programs and courses that challenge them (honors courses, for example), not simply test out because they know as much without even taking a course or by reading a book as the average student who has taken the course. What's so great, he asks, about an average knowledge of a subject? Isn't average a synonym for mediocre?

In high school, some youngsters walk into American history in September with more knowledge than other students have when they walk out in June. Should high schools simply excuse these students from American history, or should they receive a more sophisticated and challenging course than the rest? Some ninth-graders have as great a fund of general academic competency and skill as the average graduating senior. Should high schools graduate these ninth-graders, or should they retain them and offer courses commensurate with their abilities?

This may be hard for some people to believe, but I'm positive that I deal with certain high-school students who are far more knowledgeable than the average college graduate—not in a discipline such as engineering that they haven't been exposed to, but certainly in the liberal arts, which many colleges pride themselves on. Well, then, why don't we hand them a bachelor of arts degree along with their high-school diploma?

Is this really what we want? Will a country that requires merely an average knowledge of a discipline continue to produce William F. Buckleys and John Kenneth Galbraiths? Is mediocrity our objective? It's one thing to end up with it, another to actually aim for it.

On the other hand, it can be persuasively argued that our society offers economic rewards based simply on college credits and degrees. To qualify for certain jobs or increases in pay employees frequently must present college credentials. This situation is so widespread that fake degrees and degree mills have begun to plague the field of education. (One ploy is to pretend that you graduated from a college that later folded.) If college credentials have this much economic value, is it fair to penalize the individual who hasn't sat through certain courses when he is in fact the objective equal of the average person who has?

The foregoing is an educational dilemma. One can listen to both sides and agree with everything. Be that as it may, both AP and CLEP offer opportunities that many students would be wise to consider.

NONTRADITIONAL EDUCATION

Now here's an option that's an option! Would you rather take tests than courses? Would you like to receive credit for college-level education that you acquired outside of books or a classroom? There are colleges that do this and more, and they're far cheaper than traditional colleges. Some will grant you a degree even if you've never seen the inside of a college classroom in your life. And they're fully accredited, not degree mills.

REGENTS EXTERNAL DEGREES OF THE UNIVERSITY OF THE STATE OF NEW YORK

Since 1971, more than eleven thousand people from all over America have earned Regents External Degrees, and twenty thousand more are working now toward that goal. Credit toward this degree may be earned in the following ways:

1. College courses taken for degree credit from regionally accredited colleges and universities, completed either on campus or through correspondence
2. Proficiency examinations. The following are the approved current tests:
   - New York College-Proficiency Examinations (generally available in other states as ACT PEP Tests)
   - Regents External-Degree Examinations (generally available elsewhere as ACT PEP Tests)
   - Advanced-Placement (College Board) Examinations
   - CLEP (College-Level Examination Program)
   - DANTES (Defense Activity for Non-Traditional Education Support Test)
   - Graduate Record Examination Advanced Test
   - Undergraduate Assessment Program Field Test
   - United States Armed Forces Institute Test
3. Military service school courses, tests, and occupational specialties evaluated and recommended for college credit
4. Special assessment of knowledge gained from experience, independent study, or other nontraditional approaches to education
5. Noncollegiate-sponsored instruction that has been evaluated and recommended for college credit by the New York State Education Department's Office on Noncollegiate Sponsored Instruction, by the American Council on Education, by the Consortium of the California State University and Colleges, or by the Pennsylvania Department of Education
6. Federal Aviation Administration (FAA)—formerly

Civil Aeronautics Administration (CAA)—Airman
Certificates
7. A combination of these ways

The Regents External-Degree Program itself offers
no courses. It merely awards credit based on any of
these acceptable methods of accumulating credit, and
when the student has fulfilled the requirements for a
degree, he is awarded one.

Sometimes this can create some extreme situations.
For instance, suppose a student jumped from college
to college and didn't attend his last institution long
enough to qualify for its degree. If he met the graduation requirements of the Regents External-Degree
Program, he could have his transcript sent to them
and get a degree immediately.

Although most of the students enrolled in this program are in their thirties, it is available to anyone. In
fact, even if he hasn't graduated from high school, a
New York resident may receive a high-school equiva-
lency diploma after accumulating twenty-four credits
toward a degree.

The Regents External-Degree Program offers eight
degrees—in Arts, in Science, in Science (Nursing), and
in Applied Science (Nursing)—four on the associate
level and four on the baccalaureate level. It should be
noted that while the Regents External Degree is accredited by the highest accrediting agency, even this
may be insufficient in certain instances, nursing, for
example. Some state boards of nursing have not en-
dorsed the program, so students should check the
situation in each state.

Students interested in obtaining more information
should write to Regents External Degrees, The University of the State of New York, Cultural Education
Center, Albany, New York 12230.

THOMAS A. EDISON STATE COLLEGE

Thomas A. Edison State College, in New Jersey, was founded in 1972, and over fifteen hundred students have received degrees so far. In general, Edison College operates much like the Regents External-Degree Program. Credit can be earned in a variety of ways, and the college offers no classes. But it does offer a free counseling service in various parts of New Jersey.

Thomas A. Edison College awards the following degrees: the bachelor of arts degree, the bachelor of science degree with concentrations in either the human or technical services, the bachelor of science degree in business administration, and three associate, or two-year, degrees in liberal arts, management, and radiologic technology.

Interested students should write to Thomas A. Edison State College, Kelsey Building, 101 West State Street, Trenton, New Jersey 08625.

Two additional states, Connecticut and Illinois, have external-degree programs similar to New York and New Jersey, although Illinois does require at least fifteen credits of normal classroom attendance for a degree. Their addresses are Board for State Academic Awards, 340 Capitol Avenue, Hartford, Connecticut 06115 and Board of Governors BA Program, 544 Iles Park Place, Springfield, Illinois 62706.

Although programs such as these are open to anyone, they are fundamentally intended for adult learners who are unable or unwilling to devote four years of their lives to pursuing undergraduate degrees. For instance, Regents External-Degree literature describes how a talented young man from Brooklyn spent his time organizing unions and political campaigns while most people his age attended college.

When eventually he decided that he needed a law degree, he found that no law school would accept him because he lacked an undergraduate degree, even though he had scored in the top 1 percent on the Law School Admissions Test. In just nine months he was able to fulfill the bachelor of arts requirements through the Regents External-Degree Program and was then accepted by Harvard Law School. Of course, this young man was highly talented and obtained his degree with unusual speed, but his example does illustrate the potential of the Regents program.

One intriguing aspect of these programs is that they grant credit for college-level knowledge acquired through jobs or life experience. For instance, Thomas A. Edison literature described one married woman with three children who enrolled in a bachelor's degree program. This woman taught ballet at a private dance school, art at a county college, exercise therapy to a senior citizens' group, and coordinated a preschool program in creative movement. To retain her position at the college, she needed a college degree. Because of her abilities in the fields of art and dance, the college was able to grant this woman fifty-seven credits (forty-two in art and fifteen in dance) for life experience. These credits greatly speeded up the process by which she was able to obtain her degree and saved her considerable money, too.

There are major advantages to enrolling at these institutions. First, the costs will be low. Second, a student could hold a job, even a full-time one, and study for exams at his own pace. Third, a degree could be obtained more quickly. Fourth, a student isn't bound to one locale. He can move around the country or even the world and continue working toward his degree.

11

OTHER SAVINGS STRATEGIES

CONSIDERING GEOGRAPHY

Both tuition and living conditions are cheaper in certain sections of the country. In general, the most expensive regions are New England and the West; least expensive are the South and Southwest. Students might keep this in mind when they search for a college.

I have found that many students are drawn to New England, especially Boston. There is said to be a greater concentration of college students there than anywhere else in the United States (although recently Philadelphia has begun to challenge the notion, pointing out that although Boston has a greater percentage of students in comparison to its total population, the Philadelphia area actually has more students). I'm sure that Boston and New England have many charms, but keep in mind that that's Boardwalk, not Baltic Avenue. A college in the South or Southwest will cost about $1,000 to $2,000 less than an equivalent college in New England.

It must be admitted that there are more prestigious colleges in New England than in the South and Southwest put together. Massachusetts alone may have more. On the other hand, all you need is one, and New England doesn't have a monopoly on fine educational institutions.

A former counselee of mine, Kim Shafer, wrote to me about her experiences attending college in the South. After graduating in 1975 from Haverford Senior High in Pennsylvania, Kim attended Vanderbilt University in Tennessee on a prestigious no-need scholarship. While there she earned many honors, including Phi Beta Kappa membership, and served on student-faculty committees and in student government. Here is Kim's letter:

I had never been South of Williamsburg, Virginia, before starting at Vanderbilt. I have gained so much from the experience that I wish more students would venture out of the parochial Northeast. Obviously, the primary advantage of attending a Southern school (other things being equal) is the broadening experience you will gain by experiencing a different culture. People are friendlier and more traditional (more family-oriented, more courteous, etc.). By seeing a somewhat different way of life, I have learned what I do not like and what I do like about Northern ways. I have become more whole, more human, from the experience. In addition to the lure of Southern hospitality and Southern cooking is the undeniable attraction of warmer weather. You still need a winter coat, but winters are short and rarely bitter. A lower cost of living also makes the South pleasant. Eating out in Nashville is relatively inexpensive, cheap when compared to Philadelphia. My final reason for suggesting the South is probably the most important, particularly in the long run. The South's economy is expanding rapidly while the Northeast's is declining. Many people are moving to the South (or the Sunbelt) because of superior job

opportunities. Attending college in the South would en-
hance business dealings or make a relocation much
easier.

I came to Vanderbilt with all the typical prejudices
about the South, that it is racist and backward, that the
people are dumb and uncultured, that Nashville is a
country-music hicktown. Those prejudices were, like
most prejudices, based on half-truths and generally
wrong. At this point, there are probably more racists in
the North than the South. Many Vanderbilt students are
from small Southern towns, but they attend the Nashville Symphony, local theater, and the myriad of cultural
events on campus. Few Vandy students are country-
music buffs, although bluegrass, a significant cut above
country, is popular. Nashville is a financial center for the
Mid-South; it is growing, has much big business, and will
soon have a new Performing Arts Center.

Vanderbilt is a terrific place to go to college. It provides
the best in a liberal-arts education, whereas other schools
have lost sight of what it means to be an educated person.
Vanderbilt has a unique seminar program for freshmen,
and unique course offerings for relating science and the
humanities and for integrating the humanities. The bal-
ance between the social (and the extracurricular) and the
academic is better than at other pressure-cooker schools.
(Pre-meds will share notes at Vanderbilt rather than
sabotage each other's experiments.) A strong sense of
student involvement and a certain friendly atmosphere
are also important aspects of what Vanderbilt life is
about. Only 60 percent of Vandy students are from the
South or Southwest and only 45 percent are Greek, so
there is no problem with being Northern or independent
(nonfraternity/nonsorority).

I could go on for several pages more about what I like
about Vanderbilt, but I am not sure that more words
would give a substantially better picture. Plane fare is not

cheap, but I strongly recommend a campus visit. I believe that V.U. costs about $1,000 less than the Ivy League Schools (and the quality of education is comparable, better in several cases), so that the cost of a few round-trips is manageable. Vanderbilt, for reasons I do not understand, is not very well known in the Philadelphia area, although it attracts many students from New Jersey and New York. Among educators it is known and well-respected. Its nursing, medical, and divinity schools are among the best in the country. The college of arts and sciences and the law school are at the top level. In the South, Vanderbilt and Duke are the best universities. I think Vanderbilt is a nicer place to be an undergraduate. In sum, I think Vanderbilt is one of the best places to go to college because it will enable you to be better-educated and a better human being.

Kim would have been more correct had she said that the Ivy League schools are $2,000 a year more expensive, and some are closer to $3,000. Otherwise, she makes a good case for trying the South in general and Vanderbilt in particular, although it is not the intention of this writer to single out Vanderbilt. There are many good buys for families willing to search farther afield.

COMMUTING

One of the most popular means of saving money is by commuting to college. Whether a student commutes or lives on campus, the education is the same, and sometimes large savings are possible. In spite of the economic advantages, there are certain drawbacks.

First, for many families there are few if any colleges located close by. In many parts of the U.S. there are very few choices, and these may or may not be suitable institutions. Second, the savings may be mostly illusory. If a student can get a ride to college with a friend or if his father drops him off on the way to work, that's fine, but he may have to pay for a car and all of its expenses. Third, it's inconvenient traveling back and forth constantly, frequently missing campus events and occasionally lacking ready access to the library.

I myself both commuted and lived on campus. In my freshman year, when I was a commuter, my mother gave me a ride to a friend's house each morning, and my friend then took me the rest of the way to school. Since our schedules didn't mesh, I had to take the train home in the afternoon. Traveling took slightly more than half an hour in the morning and about an hour at night, depending upon connections.

I usually didn't remain on campus after my last class, since I had no room to return to. One can spend only so much time in a library or student center. If my last class ended at 2:00 P.M., I never felt like remaining until 8:00 P.M., when a famous person might be scheduled to speak, nor did I ever return home at 2:00 P.M. and then make another round-trip that night just to hear the speech. Consequently, outside of class, my involvement with the school was minimal. My social life continued to revolve around high-school friends who were also commuting to colleges in the area.

When I was finally able to get dormitory space and began living on campus, my life changed completely. All of a sudden my social crowd became my college friends, mostly from the section of the dorm in which I lived. If there was a movie on campus, a basketball game, a speaker, I could be there. I didn't even bother going home on weekends. College became my life.

Unless a student lacks the maturity to handle a college experience away from home, I feel that commuting may be one of the poorest ways to save money. College is a time when children need the opportunity to develop more independence. Parents can continue to see them during vacations and on occasional weekends, and also pay the bills. Some of the apron strings are cut, but not all. That's not too bad a situation.

GOING CHEAP, GRADUATING EXPENSIVE

Another way of cutting costs considerably is to attend an inexpensive college for a couple of years and then transfer to a more prestigious one in order to receive a degree. For instance, a student could begin at a local community college, which would be very inexpensive compared to most "name" colleges, and then transfer for the last two years.

Usually the switch has to be made after two years, since most prestigious schools want a couple of years of tuition before they'll confer a degree. In fact, a lot of the lower-status schools do, too. There are a few exceptions. Recently I was talking to a parent whose daughter wanted to transfer after her junior year; he had discovered a well-respected private college that was willing to accept and allow her to graduate in just one year. This is unusual, though.

If a student can locate a satisfactory but inexpensive college for the first two years, this could be an excellent strategy. In most majors the first few years of college are spent in introductory courses, many of them conducted in large lecture halls. If the professor at the community or state college is good, his course might be every bit as fine as a similar one at a famous institution, or perhaps better. Some of the most prestigious professors can't teach well; they have made their reputations outside of teaching.

By junior year, students begin to specialize, and a wide variety of course offerings becomes desirable. Class size also becomes more meaningful. It's insignificant whether a lecture hall has 100, 150, or 200 students, but it does matter in advanced courses whether there are 15 or 30 in a discussion group. If we're establishing priorities, there's no escaping the fact that the last two are the key years.

If a student plans on graduate school, another way to save money is to attend an inexpensive college as an undergraduate and then obtain a graduate degree from a famous university. For instance, I recall counseling a student with an outstanding record. Most students with records like his think of nothing but the most famous colleges and universities, but he was interested solely in the main campus of Penn State. When I inquired, he explained that he eventually wanted an MBA degree but that his parents couldn't finance both an expensive undergraduate and graduate program. They had concluded that it was crucial for his graduate degree to come from the prestigious institution. Eventually he planned to apply to Harvard and Penn, but in the meantime Penn State was okay.

What this young man did made considerable sense. As the reader may have noticed, I lack enthusiasm for expensive degrees unless families either can or absolutely can't afford them. The two exceptions I might make are an MBA program and law school, since the top institutions in those fields could make a major difference in career advancement.

GETTING A JOB WITH A COLLEGE

Many colleges grant the children of an employee free tuition, and frequently they also work out trades and take each other's children, giving everyone a wider choice of colleges. Some even reimburse an employee up to the cost of their own tuition if he elects to send his child elsewhere.

In one way or another colleges manage to defray the bulk of the costs of college for most of their employees, and this usually applies to both professionals and nonprofessionals. I have met parents whose principal rationale for working for a college or university was the anticipated saving on tuition. And this makes a lot of sense. Although in most cases the salaries aren't particularly impressive, colleges are pleasant places to work at, and not only is tuition free, it's tax free. For instance, how much would a family have to earn before taxes to equal, say, $6,000 a year of free tuition? Depending upon the family, it might be $8,000 or $10,000, or even more. For families with a number of children to educate, we could be talking a lot of money, usually far more than a parent might conceivably earn by accepting a better-paying job elsewhere.

Of course, there are a few horror stories. Sometimes the employee's college is too competitive for his child, and no agreement exists with a less demanding one. Many parents become frantic when this occurs, since they face substantial costs at an inferior institution if their child is rejected. There's some phenomenal string-pulling in these cases. On the other end of the scale, students occasionally feel superior to the free college, and there are families that have spent small fortunes because their children felt this way.

It's understandable that colleges want to offer this service to their employees, but it's also ironic. Many colleges proclaim that all of their financial aid is based solely on need, and some even assume a holier-than-thou stance toward institutions offering academic and/or athletic awards. Simultaneously, these "need-only" schools offer free educations to their employees' children. If these schools truly believe that need-based aid is absolutely fair to everyone, how can this be? If a professor needs assistance in order to send his child to college, wouldn't he receive it through need-based aid? If he doesn't require assistance, doesn't offering his child a free education violate the "need-only" principle about which these schools profess to feel so strongly?

COMPANY-SPONSORED STUDY

Many corporations have tuition-aid plans covering part or all of a full-time employee's college tuition expenses. A student could begin working for such a company and have the company finance almost all of his education while he is still receiving his regular salary. Typically, such a student attends college in the evening and doesn't carry a full course load, which means that it takes him longer to graduate. Most companies wouldn't finance full-time study in any case.

American Telephone and Telegraph, to cite one representative plan, pays 100 percent of the tuition and certain other fees for up to eighteen credits per year. Books, transportation, parking fees, etc., are not covered. Also, courses not reasonably related to ATT's business and goals are not covered, which would exclude majors such as medicine and home economics.

With minor exceptions, most of the companies surveyed have similar plans. Georgia Pacific reimburses only 80 percent; Hoover allows $1,000 a year rather than eighteen credits; IBM has, in addition, a Retirement Education Assistance Plan that pays for courses for older employees who wish to develop a hobby or start a new career; Boeing also allows a doctoral candidate a one-year educational leave of absence during which time they continue to pay him half of his salary and also reimburse him for tuition and fees.

It appears that most large corporations have tuition-refund plans, although there are exceptions (Sears, for instance). It would be nice if we had a single source of information about which companies offer what, but to the best of my knowledge no such compilation has ever been made. Students who are interested can easily check with large companies that are local.

BUYING A HOUSE

Consider purchasing a house or condominium for your child or children to use while in college. One or more rooms could also be rented out to other college students. The advantages include savings on dorm fees, savings on food, since meals could be cooked at home, possible appreciation in the price of the property, possible rent, income-tax deductions for the property tax and mortgage interest, and possible tax deductions for operating a rental property. The disadvantages include taxes on the property, maintenance, utilities, mortgage payments, and getting tied down to another property (it's advantageous for all children to attend the same college, for instance).

Some people have done very well with this idea, especially when the property increases in value. Sometimes appreciation plus the other benefits covers the costs of the children's educations. In addition, I can think of one family that was able to obtain in-state tuition rates.

ONE-TIME TUITION PAYMENT

Washington University, in St. Louis, has a Tuition Stabilization Plan. If a parent pays the full four years of tuition at the time his child enters, he pays nothing more, thereby saving himself any increases in tuition. If he lacks cash, the university will lend him the money at 13 percent interest.

It's difficult to assess the value of this option, since we don't know how rapidly Washington University will increase tuition. Let's say a parent who elects the four-years-at-once plan will pay $28,500; if tuition increases by 10 percent per year, the parent who pays annually will be charged:

$$\begin{array}{r} \$7,125.00 \\ 7,837.50 \\ 8,621.25 \\ +\,9,483.38 \\ \hline \$33,067.13 \end{array}$$

The parent making a lump-sum payment will save:

$$\begin{array}{r} \$33,067.13 \\ -\ 28,500.00 \\ \hline \$\ 4,567.13 \end{array}$$

Keep in mind that in any case half of the first year's tuition ($3,562.50) would be due immediately and $3,562.50 more about four months thereafter. Also, those with assets who elect not to pay the full four years will have to pay taxes on the income they receive from those assets. Finally, those who borrow at 13 percent will be able to deduct the interest from income taxes.

The University of Southern California and Case Western Reserve have similar plans, and no doubt others will before long.

Dickinson College has established a loan plan to help parents who have been denied Guaranteed Student Loans. Any such parent presenting proof of such denial can borrow up to $2,500 a year for four years at 13 percent interest plus a 3 percent origination fee ($75 for each $2,500 loan). While the student is in college, only interest is paid, and the loan and interest are normally paid back over the next six years.

This loan could be a good idea, since a bank would charge a higher rate of interest (assuming that the loan could even be obtained in the first place). On the other hand, 13 percent interest isn't manna from heaven. Someone borrowing money through this plan will end up paying almost double what he was originally charged, although tax considerations could lessen the impact.

Fairleigh Dickinson University has a Family Plan that can save a family with several children a good deal of money. If two or more dependent children from a family attend the university simultaneously, the first pays full tuition and any others pay only half. If a husband and wife are both enrolled, one pays only half-tuition. (I wonder whether many Fairleigh Dickinson students get married while in school.) The parents and grandparents of a dependent, full-time undergraduate may take any undergraduate course tuition-free, providing class space is available.

Here's something that may be of assistance to students. Colleges and universities are expected to allow applicants to wait until May 1, or until they have heard from all of the institutions to which they have applied (whichever is earlier), before replying to an offer of admission and/or financial aid. Sometimes a student gets caught in a bind. He's accepted to a college that's not his first choice, and it demands a $100 nonrefundable deposit within thirty days, long before he'll know whether he's accepted at his first choice. Students who find themselves in this dilemma should request that their counselors notify the president of the state or regional Association of College Admissions Counselors. In addition, the student should send a copy of all correspondence to Executive Director, NACAC, 9933 Lawler Avenue, Suite 500, Skokie, Illinois 60077; or School College Relations, National Association of Secondary School Principals, 1904 Association Drive, Reston, Virginia 22091.

Students who are alert shouldn't have to waste a tuition deposit, although I can't guarantee this. They should also realize that they have responsibilities as well as rights, and should notify colleges promptly when they wish to accept or reject an offer of admission. Colleges can operate most effectively and notify more students promptly when applicants themselves act responsibly.

12

COLLEGE AND FINANCIAL-AID CHECKLIST

TENTH GRADE

Students should:

1. Apply for a social security number.
2. Investigate career information to determine which areas appear most suitable to their interests and abilities.
3. Analyze the courses they should be taking in high school to prepare for the career of their choice. A general college-prep curriculum is suitable for most but not all college majors.
4. Read college literature and visit at least one college to get an idea of what a college is.
5. Consider taking the PSAT in the fall. This test is meant for juniors but can be taken by sophomores as a warm-up exercise.

Parents should:

1. Examine their finances in the light of college costs and their chances for financial aid.
2. Discuss college financial planning with their child.
3. Expose their child to as much career information as possible. Especially valuable would be trips to busi-

197

nesses and factories where the student could see and talk to people performing various types of work.

4. Try to visit one or more colleges with their child. Often, visits to college campuses can fit in with vacation plans.

ELEVENTH GRADE

Students should:

1. Take the PSAT in the fall. This test is used to select the National Merit Scholars as well as to give students a warm-up exercise for the SAT and indicate their probable SAT scoring range.
2. Take the SAT or ACT in the spring of the year.
3. Consider taking the Achievement tests in the spring. If a college requires Achievement tests and a student wants an early decision from the college, it may be necessary to take the Achievements prior to the senior year. Also, if you are just finishing a course, you might prefer to be tested in it immediately rather than in the senior year.
4. Continue to examine career possibilities and the college majors leading to these careers.
5. Develop a list of colleges that seem appropriate, begin to find out about these colleges in depth, and try to visit them. Spring vacation and the summer after the junior year are probably the best times for visiting colleges that aren't local.
6. If you plan to request an appointment to one of the service academies (such as West Point or Annapolis), do this in the spring.
7. Meet with some of the college representatives who visit high schools, to learn more about their colleges

and to become more sophisticated about what to look for in a college.

Parents should:

1. See that their child is doing everything he should be doing, but not do it for him. Colleges are suspicious of students whose parents seem to be the driving force behind an application.
2. Review their college financial planning, since there may have been changes in their income or assets, or in the college financial-aid situation.
3. Have a conference with their child's counselor to review educational and financial matters.

TWELFTH GRADE

Students should:

1. Request applications for admissions and financial aid from colleges early in the senior year. If the objective is nursing, do it very early.
2. Meet with college representatives at the colleges themselves or at the high school, and attend one or more of the College Fairs. Many colleges attend each College Fair, so it is possible to chat with a number of representatives from colleges you may be considering.
3. Visit any colleges they may have just added to their lists.
4. See their counselor to discuss their plans and resolve any last-minute problems.
5. Apply to the college or colleges of their choice in the fall (early fall if they are Early Decision candidates). Apply early if they want to attend the main campuses of some state universities.

6. Have their parents fill out the financial-aid forms in early January.
7. Repeat the SAT in the fall and take any Achievement tests that may be required by the colleges to which they are applying (not all colleges require Achievements).
8. Take the ACT this fall if they didn't take it in the spring of their junior year. Unlike the SAT, which most students take two or three times, the ACT is meant to be taken only once. Most students take one or the other of these exams, not both.

Parents should:

1. Keep in close touch with what their child is doing in regard to college applications. Monitor what he is doing, but don't do it for him. He is the one going to college!
2. Apply for financial aid in early January, using the information given earlier in this book.

13

BEST BUYS

It never ceases to amaze me that inexpensive colleges receive widespread publicity. Magazines and newspapers frequently list them, and there's even a book published each year that is nothing but a computer printout of the least expensive institutions in the country. Such lists strike me as pointless since they inform the reader only of the price of the college and ignore completely the value of the educations offered. Some colleges may demand little, but perhaps they offer little also. There are two parts to every transaction: what you pay and what you receive for what you pay.

This section seeks to rectify these one-sided presentations by identifying those institutions that represent fine or even outstanding values. Before I included a college, I compared its cost with those of colleges offering similar educational experiences and attracting similar kinds of students. While many of the suggested schools are inexpensive, some, such as Cal Tech and Swarthmore, are rather costly compared to most universities, but they are good buys. Both offer excellent value when compared to equally prestigious schools. Even at a discount, a Cadillac would cost more than a Chevy.

To compile the list I relied partly upon personal knowledge of colleges and universities formed over sixteen years as a high-school guidance counselor. In addition, the "College Admissions Selector" from *Barron's Profiles of American Colleges*, *The Competitive Colleges* from Peterson's Guides, the *Selective Guide To Colleges 1982–83* by Edward B. Fiske, and the *Insiders Guide To Colleges 1981–82* compiled and edited by the Yale Daily News, were used to identify, categorize, and evaluate quality institutions throughout the country. *The College Cost Book 1981–82* from the College Board was the source for tuition and room and board costs. Along with these totals, I figured in basic statistics on each college: the percentage of applicants accepted, average SAT and/or ACT scores, the percentage of accepted students scoring 600 or better on the verbal and math sections of the SAT, the student-to-faculty ratio, and the number of volumes in the library.

Before you approach the list, consider some of the factors that affected its compilation:

1. Since all public colleges and universities receive tax dollars, all of them offer fine value because their students are paying only a fraction of the cost of their educations. Consequently, even though all public institutions by their very nature constitute good buys, only those that are especially noteworthy or offer inordinate value were included.
2. Only better known and higher quality institutions were evaluated. Since there are so many average colleges and universities, the bulk of them known only locally, it didn't seem worthwhile or even practicable to try to distinguish among them. Undoubtedly many of those also offer fine value.
3. Eliminating colleges from the list was a painful task. Perhaps in a given tier of colleges *A* might have been the best buy, but *B* might not have been much

higher. Since both were good buys compared to the competition, it seemed a shame to discard strong seconds. Then, too, some colleges were eliminated simply because they were too small (for example, Deep Springs College, which offers free room, board, and tuition, to every one of its twenty-five or thirty extremely talented students) or specialized (Webb Institute of Naval Architecture, for instance). Overlooking colleges such as these would be unfortunate since they could be perfect for the right student. Consequently, following this list of Twenty Best Buys I have listed forty others that also offer fine value, though they failed to make my original list.

4. Finally, no college featured as a good buy elsewhere in this book was included since this would have been redundant. The colleges listed are presented alphabetically, not according to any order of preference.

TWENTY BEST BUYS

Baylor University, Waco, Texas. Baylor is a large (8,400 undergraduates) private university affiliated with the Southern Baptists. Accordingly, Baylor has strict social rules and encourages a Christian outlook upon life. While most majors are offered, business-related ones have become the most popular.

Brigham Young University, Provo, Utah. Founded by the Church of Jesus Christ of Latter Day Saints, Brigham Young has evolved into a large (25,000 undergraduates) university that offers a fine educational experience along with a strict code of moral behavior—the use of tea, coffee, alcoholic beverages, and tobacco is prohibited.

College of William and Mary, Williamsburg, Virginia.
A state supported college, William and Mary offers a
high quality education, a beautiful campus situated in
Colonial Williamsburg, and an illustrious history (as
alma mater to three United States presidents and
birthplace of Phi Beta Kappa). Not the best kept
secret, William and Mary is very competitive in admissions, especially for the nonstate resident.

Colorado College, Colorado Springs, Colorado. A medium-size (1,850 students) private college, Colorado
College features two key attractions. First, the school
year has been divided into nine blocks, each three and
one-half weeks long, and students carry only one
course at a time during each of these blocks. Second,
Colorado College is located in the Rocky Mountains
and surrounded by natural beauty and ski resorts.

Cooper Union, New York, New York. A heavily endowed private college, Cooper Union is hard to match
since it is tuition-free. Cooper Union offers majors in
architecture, fine arts, and engineering, but its social
life is limited since it lacks dormitories and has a high
percentage of commuters.

Davidson College, Davidson, North Carolina. Davidson is a small (1,300 students) Presbyterian liberal
arts college that has an excellent academic reputation. Located in a small town that offers few diver-
sions, Davidson is most suitable for the serious student.

Emory University, Atlanta, Georgia. Long recognized
as one of the finest private Southern universities,
Emory has begun to establish an outstanding national
reputation, propelled by its huge endowments. In
1979 Robert W. Woodruff, chairman of Coca-Cola,
gave Emory $100 million in Coca-Cola stock. This was
the largest single donation in the history of American

philanthropy—and Emory ranked eighteenth nationally in endowments *before* that gift was received.

Furman University, Greenville, South Carolina. Southern Baptist affiliated and conservative, Furman nevertheless presents a vigorous academic environment on a gorgeous 750-acre campus with a 30-acre lake.

Grove City College, Grove City, Pennsylvania. United Presbyterian affiliated, Grove City is an excellent medium-size college with an attractive 150-acre campus. Heavily endowed through the generosity of J. Howard Pew of Sun Oil, Grove City has managed to keep its charges remarkably low.

New College of the University of South Florida, Sarasota, Florida. Founded as a private college, New College became the honors college of the University of South Florida in 1975. Subsequently, it retained all of the individuality for which it had previously been noted but gained the low tuition of a public college. New College is small (about 500 students), and independent study and seminars rather than lectures are stressed. Most students gain advanced standing and graduate in three years.

Rice University, Houston, Texas. One of the most prestigious universities in the nation, Rice offers excellent programs in most majors and outstanding ones in the sciences and engineering. Most of Rice's 2,500 undergraduates live on eight campus colleges, each with its own student government, social events, and intramural sports teams.

St. Olaf College, Northfield, Minnesota. St. Olaf is a 3,000-student, Lutheran affiliated liberal arts college with a strong academic program generally and an outstanding international studies program.

Swarthmore College, Swarthmore, Pennsylvania. Set

on a beautiful, suburban Philadelphia campus, Swarthmore is one of the most prestigious small liberal arts and engineering colleges in the country.

University of California, Berkeley, California. The University of California offers fine education on all of its campuses, but Berkeley is considered the most illustrious. Famous for students who march to a different drummer as well as for its academic programs, Berkeley has a diverse student population of 30,000. The profusion of ideas constantly whirling around Berkeley make it one of the most intellectually stimulating campuses.

University of Michigan, Ann Arbor, Michigan. A large (35,000 undergraduates) state university, Michigan is justly famous for its fine academic programs and illustrious professors as well as for its football team.

University of North Carolina, Chapel Hill, North Carolina. Set on a beautiful campus and offering an appealing life-style as well as a top-notch public education, North Carolina's main branch has attracted many admirers. Consequently, out-of-state applicants need strong credentials for admission.

University of Notre Dame, Notre Dame, Indiana. While Notre Dame is justly famous for its football team, people sometimes forget that academically it is also one of the two most outstanding Catholic universities in the United States. Solid in most majors, Notre Dame is probably strongest in science and engineering.

University of Texas, Austin, Texas. More frequently noted for its football teams than its academic offerings, the University of Texas is in the process of changing its image. And it will be able to do so because it owns two million acres of oil-producing land donated to it by the state in 1883. The most heavily endowed institution of higher education in the country, the university has been using this revenue wisely. Many millions of dollars have been spent on facilities, famous professors have been and are being hired, and standards of admission are being raised. The University of Texas will be heard from in the years ahead, and not just on the football field.

University of Virginia, Charlottesville, Virginia. Founded by Thomas Jefferson, who also designed its grounds and original buildings, the University of Virginia is a state university with a historic past, a stimulating academic environment, a lively social life, and possibly the most beautiful campus in the country.

Wake Forest University, Winston-Salem, North Carolina. Located since 1956 on the former estate of a tobacco baron, Wake Forest offers an excellent liberal arts education in a magnificent setting of trees, shrubs, and gardens.

FORTY ADDITIONAL GOOD BUYS

Agnes Scott College, Decatur, Georgia
Coe College, Cedar Rapids, Iowa
Colorado School of Mines, Golden, Colorado (in state
    only)
De Paul University, Chicago, Illinois
Deep Springs College, Deep Springs, California
Duke University, Durham, North Carolina
Florida Institute of Technology, Melbourne, Florida
Georgetown University, Washington, D.C.
George Washington University, Washington, D.C.
Georgia Institute of Technology, Atlanta, Georgia
Guilford College, Greensboro, North Carolina
Hanover College, Hanover, Indiana

Houghton College, Houghton, New York
Howard University, Washington, D.C.
Illinois Institute of Technology, Chicago, Illinois
Indiana University, Bloomington, Indiana
Johns Hopkins University, Baltimore, Maryland
Le Moyne College, Syracuse, New York
Mary Washington College, Fredericksburg, Virginia
Massachusetts Maritime Academy, Buzzards Bay, Massachusetts
Miami University, Oxford, Ohio
Rose-Hulman Institute of Technology, Terre Haute, Indiana
Saint John's University, Collegeville, Minnesota
State University of New York (SUNY) at Albany, Binghamton, Buffalo, and Stony Brook, New York
Texas Christian University, Fort Worth, Texas
University of Dallas, Irving, Texas
University of Illinois, Champaign-Urbana, Illinois
University of Iowa, Iowa City, Iowa
University of Kansas, Lawrence, Kansas
University of Richmond, Richmond, Virginia
University of Washington, Washington
University of Wisconsin, Madison, Wisconsin
Ursinus College, Collegeville, Pennsylvania
Virginia Polytechnic Institute and State University, Blacksburg, Virginia
Washington and Lee University, Lexington, Virginia
Webb Institute of Naval Architecture, Glen Cove, New York
Wheaton College, Wheaton, Illinois
Whitman College, Walla Walla, Washington
Yeshiva University, New York, New York

Appendix

LIST OF "NO-NEED" SCHOLARSHIPS

Here is a list of merit scholarships that are awarded without regard to financial need. Keep in mind that there are over three thousand colleges and universities in the United States, many of which are constantly establishing merit awards for the first time, adding new merit awards to existing ones, or increasing the value of existing awards. This list is a good place to begin, but if your favorite college is missing, find out whether it actually does offer merit scholarships.

Note also that some schools do in effect offer these scholarships even though they claim otherwise. For instance, one institution dislikes losing students to colleges that are its peers or better. If they discover that an applicant has received an attractive offer from a competitor, they'll match it. If the offer came from an inferior school, however, they'd do nothing. Don't be afraid to talk to people who can help you. When a college wants a student badly enough, things can happen if the financial-aid office is alerted to the dilemma.

Adams State College, Alamosa, Colorado—Honors at Entrance Scholarships worth $500 a year plus a room for one year only: applicants must be in top 10 percent of class and have an ACT score of 21 or SAT score of 950.

Adelphi University, Garden City, New York—Trustee Scholarship worth one-third of tuition each year: top tenth of class. Also, other academic awards, plus awards in art and performing arts.

University of Alabama, Tuscaloosa, Alabama—Alumni Honors worth $1,000 a year: top 10 percent plus good SAT.

Alderson-Broaddus College, Philippi, West Virginia—Up to $2,750 per year.

Alfred University, Alfred, New York—Scholarships in history, philosophy, and religion: $500 per year for best essays on these subjects.

Allegheny College, Meadville, Pennsylvania—Twenty-four scholarships of $500 per year based on a competitive exam.

Alma College, Alma, Michigan—Trustee Scholarship worth $1,500 per year: top tenth plus 29 ACT.

American University, Washington, D.C.—American University Scholarship worth half tuition: top twentieth, 1200 SAT. Presidential Scholarship worth $1,000: top tenth plus 1000 SAT.

Ashland College, Ashland, Ohio—Three scholarships covering full tuition, and room and board, plus seven covering full tuition, based purely on a test administered at the college.

Avila College, Kansas City, Missouri—Scholarships worth up to $3,100 per year.

Baldwin-Wallace College, Berea, Ohio—Scholarships worth $500 per year based on academics (top 15 percent plus good SAT or ACT) or talent in areas such as theater or art. Scholarships in music worth up to $1,000 per year.

Ball State University, Muncie, Indiana—Whitinger Scholarship worth full tuition plus $200: want top tenth plus 1200 SAT.

Barry College, Miami Shores, Florida—Thirty-five Presidential Scholarships worth one-quarter to one-third tuition each year: academic potential and leadership.

Beaver College, Glenside, Pennsylvania—Four Arts Scholarships worth $1,000 each per year.

Beloit College, Beloit, Wisconsin—Ten Presidential Scholarships worth $2,000 each per year: top tenth plus strong SAT or ACT.

Bentley College, Waltham, Massachusetts—One hundred $1,000 scholarships per year.

Berry College, Mount Berry, Georgia—Numerous academic scholarships: B average plus above-average SAT.

Bethany College, Bethany, West Virginia—Honors Scholarship worth $2,500 per year.

Bowling Green State University, Bowling Green, Ohio—President's Scholarship worth half tuition: 1300 SAT or 29 ACT. Also other scholarships.

Boston University, Boston, Massachusetts—Full tuition: 3.7 GPA, top 5 percent of class, plus 1300 in SAT or 700 in one half.

Bradley University, Peoria, Illinois—Several scholarships up to 50 percent of tuition.

Brigham Young University, Provo, Utah—Academic scholarships for students who have about a 3.5 GPA or better plus high SAT. Best scholarship, Spencer W. Kimball, open only to members of the Church of Jesus Christ of Latter-Day Saints, worth up to $2,000 a year.

C. W. Post Center of Long Island University, Greenvale, New York—Academic Performance Awards worth $1,000 per year: 85 high-school average plus 900 SAT. Academic Excellence Awards worth $500 plus the $1,000 for the Academic Performance Awards: 90 high-school average plus 1100 SAT.

Caldwell College, Caldwell, New Jersey—Both full-tuition and half-tuition academic scholarships.

University of California, Irvine, California—Chancellors Club scholarships worth $1,000 per year.

California Institute of Technology, Pasadena, California—Prize scholarships worth $750 to $1,500 per year: all applicants to college automatically considered.

California State College, Bakersfield, California—Scholarships worth $1,500 each a year.

California State College, California, Pennsylvania—Academic scholarships: top 5 percent plus SAT over 1200. Recent awards worth $2,000 each.

California State College, San Bernardino, California—A. F. Moore Scholarships worth $1,200 each per year.

California State University, Los Angeles, California—Freshman Honor Scholarships worth $500 each per year.

Calvin College, Grand Rapids, Michigan—Several scholarships worth up to $550.

Campbell College, Buies Creek, North Carolina—Competitive scholarships awarded for academic excellence.

Capital University, Columbus, Ohio—Presidential Scholarship worth $1,300 per year: top twentieth of class plus 1300 SAT or 29 ACT; also a number of other academic and music scholarships (instrumental and vocal).

Carleton College, Northfield, Minnesota—National Merit Semifinalist/Finalist receives automatic $500/$1,000 per year.

Case Western Reserve University, Cleveland, Ohio—Case Institute of Technology: eighteen full-tuition scholarships through Albert W. Smith and Horsburgh Scholarships (exam and interview required). Western Reserve College: five full-tuition through Andrew Squire Scholarship. Also, twenty half-tuition to Case and twenty to Western Reserve.

Catawba College, Salisbury, North Carolina—Academic scholarships; also, automatic $500 reduction for children of ministers of the United Church of Christ.

Centenary College, Shreveport, Louisiana—Two $1,120 scholarships plus two half-tuition.

Central College, Pella, Iowa—Five Rolscreen Scholars per year for award worth $2,000 per year; other awards to $1,650.

College of Charleston, Charleston, South Carolina—Academic scholarships worth $1,000 per year: top twentieth plus 1000 SAT.

University of Charleston, Charleston, West Virginia—Full tuition for high-school valedictorians and salutatorians, and National Merit Finalists. Also, students with B averages or higher can receive from $500 to $1,500 per year.

Chatham College, Pittsburgh, Pennsylvania—Five Merit Scholarships worth $2,000 each: based on academics, activities, and intellectual promise.

Chestnut Hill College, Philadelphia, Pennsylvania—Presidential Scholarships worth full tuition: based on achievement, SAT, recommendations, and activities.

University of Cincinnati, Cincinnati, Ohio—Merit awards worth up to $2,900 per year.

Coe College, Cedar Rapids, Iowa—Presidential and Fine Arts Scholarships worth $1,500 per year.

Colorado School of Mines, Golden, Colorado—Several types of scholarships, most reserved for Colorado residents.

University of Connecticut, Storrs, Connecticut—University scholarships worth full tuition.

Converse College, Spartanburg, South Carolina—Five scholarships worth $2,500 per year each: must pursue a bachelor of arts or a bachelor of fine arts major; bachelor of music isn't included.

Cornell College, Mount Vernon, Iowa—King Scholarships worth $1,000 per year and Presidential Scholarships worth $500 per year.

Creighton University, Omaha, Nebraska—Academic scholarships from $150 per year to half tuition.

University of Dallas, Dallas, Texas—Full tuition: must apply early in fall and take private test.

David Lipscomb College, Nashville, Tennessee—Honor, academic, special achievement, and athletic scholarships.

Davis and Elkins College, Elkins, West Virginia—Honor Scholarships worth $300 without need: top tenth of class.

University of Dayton, Dayton, Ohio—Over 200 scholarships per year ranging from $200 to $4,400 per year: top 10 percent plus 1100 or better SAT.

DePaul University, Chicago, Illinois—Scholarships worth up to $1,500 a year: strong grades plus 1200 SAT or 30 ACT.

DePauw University, Greencastle, Indiana—Honor Scholarships worth $1,500 per year: top 5 percent of class, outstanding qualities of character and leadership.

Dean Junior College, Franklin, Massachusetts—Academic scholarships.

University of Delaware, Newark, Delaware—Thirty-five scholarships per year worth $500 to $1,000 each per year: 3.5 GPA plus 1300 SAT.

Delaware Valley College, Doylestown, Pennsylvania—Honors Scholarship Program worth $500 per year.

Denison University, Granville, Ohio—Several awards, up to $1,000.

University of Denver, Denver, Colorado—Six Alumni Scholarships per year worth full tuition; Honors Program Scholarships worth half tuition; University Scholars Scholarships worth $1,500 per year: top 15 percent for this, but higher for first two awards.

University of Detroit, Detroit, Michigan—Ten Insignis Scholarships per year worth full tuition: top 10 percent, 95 percent on SAT or ACT, extracurricular activities; also partial scholarships.

Drew University, Madison, New Jersey—Forty Merit Scholarships worth $1,500 each per year: academic excellence, written examination, community service.

Duke University, Durham, North Carolina—Angier B. Duke Memorial Scholarships worth $6,000 per year plus a six-week free summer session at New College, Oxford University, England.

Duquesne University, Pittsburgh, Pennsylvania—University Scholars Awards: for exceptional scholars; amount not stated.

D'Youville College, Buffalo, New York—Academic scholarships for B or better average plus at least 1050 SAT.

Earlham College, Richmond, Indiana—Honors Scholarship worth $1,000 per year: top tenth plus 1100 SAT.

Eastern College, St. Davids, Pennsylvania—Four Presidential Scholarships worth $2,500 each per year, four Honors Scholarships worth $1,000 each per year: leadership, scholastic achievement, Christian service; top tenth plus 1100 SAT or 27 ACT.

Eastern Michigan University, Ypsilanti, Michigan—Regents Scholarship worth $1,200 per year: good grades plus 1050 SAT or 24 ACT.

Eckerd College, St. Petersburg, Florida—Five Presidential Scholarships a year worth $2,500 each per year; forty Honors Scholarships worth $2,000 each per year; Achievement Scholarships worth $2,000 per year for outstanding achievement in areas such as an academic subject, a creative art, athletics, or service to school or community.

Eisenhower College of RIT, Seneca Falls, New York—Merit scholarships worth as much as $1,500.

Elizabethtown College, Elizabethtown, Pennsylvania—Twelve Presidential Scholarships per year worth $1,000 to $4,000 per year: high achievement plus 1100 SAT. Other awards from $200 to $1,000: top 10 percent plus 1000 SAT.

Elmira College, Elmira, New York—Merit scholarships worth up to $1,000.

Elmhurst College, Elmhurst, Illinois—Freshman Scholarship worth $1,000 per year.

Emory and Henry College, Emory, Virginia—Academic scholarships worth up to $750 per year.

Emory University, Atlanta, Georgia—Twelve Robert W. Woodruff Scholarships per year, each worth $7,500 per year: must be nominated by high school and have outstanding qualifications.

University of Evansville, Evansville, Illinois—President's Scholarship worth $1,000 per year: top twentieth plus 1100 SAT and 24 ACT.

Fairleigh Dickinson University, Madison, Rutherford, and Teaneck, New Jersey—Family Plan: first child pays full tuition, others who attend simultaneously pay only half tuition.

Fisk University, Nashville, Tennessee—Honors Scholarship worth $1,500 per year.

University of Florida, Gainesville, Florida—National Merit Scholars sponsored for at least $500 per year; one offered to every Finalist who has named the University as a first choice. Also athletic and music scholarships.

Florida State University, Tallahassee, Florida—Honors Scholarships for Florida residents; out-of-state students with 3.5 GPA and 1200 SAT or 27 ACT can enter Honors Program and receive partial tuition waiver (currently worth about $276 per quarter).

Fordham University, New York, New York—Presidential Scholarship worth $5,500: top tenth, 1300 SAT.

Franklin College, Franklin, Indiana—President's Scholarship worth $1,500 a year, Ben Franklin Scholarship worth $1,000 a year.

Franklin Pierce College, Rindge, New Hampshire—Merit scholarships in academic, artistic, and athletic areas.

Furman University, Greenville, South Carolina—Several kinds of Honors Scholarships "to encourage students of excellent character who possess exceptional scholastic ability."

Gannon College, Erie, Pennsylvania—Alumni Scholarship worth $200 to $2,000; others worth $100 to $600.

Geneva College, Beaver Falls, Pennsylvania—Honor Scholarships worth $300 per year for top tenth of class, $150 per year for top fifth.

George Peabody College for Teachers, Nashville, Tennessee—Peabody Scholars Program offers $1,000, $1,500, or $2,500 per year: 3.5 GPA for $2,500; 3.0 for $1,000 or $1,500.

George Washington University, Washington, D.C.—Scholarships worth $1,000 per year: top 5 or 10 percent, 1250 SAT. Half-tuition awards from School of Engineering and Applied Science.

University of Georgia, Athens, Georgia—National Merit and Achievement Scholarships worth minimum of $500 per year. Freshman Alumni Scholarships worth $500 per year: B average plus high SAT; Alumni Foundation Fellowships worth $2,500 per year: excellent records plus 1400+ SAT.

Grand Canyon College, Phoenix, Arizona—Academic and fine-arts scholarships worth $600 to $900 per year.

Grand Valley State College, Allendale, Michigan—Presidential Scholarships worth $1,500 per year; Honor Scholarships worth $500 per year.

Green Mountain College, Poultney, Vermont—Scholars Program worth $500 per semester first year, $1,000 per semester second year, $1,500 per semester third and fourth years: top 15 percent, SAT of 1200.

Guilford College, Greensboro, North Carolina—Scholarships worth $1,000 per year: top tenth plus 1250 SAT.

University of Hartford, West Hartford, Connecticut—Academic Scholarships: top 10 percent plus 1100 SAT; also Talent Scholarships in Art and Music and some Athletic Grants.

Hartwick College, Oneonta, New York—Academic Merit Scholarships worth $1,000 per year.

Heidelberg College, Tiffin, Ohio—Trustee Scholarships worth $1,000 for one year only.

High Point College, High Point, North Carolina—Presidential Scholarship worth $1,250 per year; Honor worth $750 per year; Merit worth $500 per year: top quarter plus good SAT.

Hillsdale College, Hillsdale, Michigan—Three Distinct Honor Scholarships worth full tuition: top 5 percent of class and on SAT or ACT; ten Presidential Scholarships worth $1,750 per year: top 10 percent; twenty Trustee Scholarships worth $1,500 per year: top 20 percent; fifty Achievement Scholarships worth $800 to $1,200 per year: top 25 percent of class.

Hiram College, Hiram, Ohio—Honor scholarships worth up to $1,000 per year.

Hofstra University, Hempstead, New York—Memorial Honors Scholarships worth $1,500: top 5 percent plus 1350 SAT; Distinguished Academic Scholarships worth $800: top 20 percent plus 1200 SAT; Freshman Recognition Scholarships worth $500: top 10 percent plus 1000 to 1199 SAT.

Hood College, Frederick, Maryland—Automatic $500 per year for students who achieve National Merit Commended or higher; also Hobson Beneficial Scholarship worth from one third to two thirds of tuition.

Houston Baptist University, Houston, Texas—Full- and half-tuition academic scholarships, plus half-tuition nursing, ministerial, and music-major scholarships.

Howard University, Washington, D.C.—Full-tuition academic scholarships.

University of Houston, Houston, Texas—Academic awards worth up to $2,500 per year.

Illinois Institute of Technology, Chicago, Illinois—Presidential

Scholarship worth $1,000 per year: want top tenth plus 1200 SAT or 28 ACT.

Indiana State University, Terre Haute, Indiana—Has academic scholarships for students in top 10 percent of class.

Indiana University of Pennsylvania, Indiana, Pennsylvania—Fifteen Distinguished Achiever Scholarships per year worth $1,000 per year: top tenth plus 1100 on SAT.

Johns Hopkins University, Baltimore, Maryland—Scholarship worth $1,500 per year: outstanding achievement.

Juniata College, Huntingdon, Pennsylvania—Academic Achievement Scholarships: test at Juniata on humanities, social sciences, and natural sciences; winners awarded either Brumbaugh-Ellis Presidential Scholarships worth $1,500 per year (top tenth of class plus good SAT) or Alumni Annual Support Scholarships worth $1,000 per year (good record).

University of Kansas, Lawrence, Kansas—Several kinds of honor scholarships.

King's College, Wilkes-Barre, Pennsylvania—Honors and Presidential Scholarships worth up to $6,000.

Knox College, Galesburg, Illinois—Presidential Scholarship worth $2,000 per year, academic achievement scholarship worth $500 per year.

LaSalle College, Philadelphia, Pennsylvania—At least thirty full-tuition scholarships per year: top fifth of class, plus 1300 SAT; applicants must also write 500-word personal essay.

Lebanon Valley College, Annville, Pennsylvania—Full-tuition Presidential Scholarships: top quarter of class, 1000 SAT, plus high score on Lebanon Valley exam.

Lehigh University, Bethlehem, Pennsylvania—Ten Presidential Prizes worth $1,000 per year: unusual leadership qualities; also sponsors National Merit Scholarships worth at least $500 per year.

Lock Haven State College, Lock Haven, Pennsylvania—Band

Scholarships: must have been in high-school band and have acceptable SAT and class rank; need not major in music.

Long Island University, Brooklyn Center, Brooklyn, New York—Full-tuition academic scholarships.

Longwood College, Farmville, Virginia—Scholarships for valedictorians, salutatorians, and National Merit Commended students; also Performance Scholarships in art, music, and athletics.

Loyola University, New Orleans, Louisiana—Presidential Scholarship worth $3,200 per year: top 15 percent plus 1300 SAT or 28 ACT; also awards worth $1,000 per year.

Luther College, Decorah, Iowa—Regents Scholarship worth $750 per year: top tenth, 1250 SAT or 28 ACT; Luther College Scholarship worth $400 per year: top 15 percent plus 1150 SAT or 26 ACT.

Lycoming College, Williamsport, Pennsylvania—Freshman Recognition Scholarships worth $700 per year; other scholarships ranging up to full tuition for students with strong credentials: at least top fifth and 1100 or better SAT.

Lynchburg College, Lynchburg, Virginia—T. Brady Saunders Honor Scholarships worth $1,000 per year: top tenth of class, SAT of 1000; Hopwood Scholarships: high school juniors in top fifth of class attend one-week summer course at Lynchburg and receive one college credit; most outstanding receive four-year scholarships worth $1,000 per year.

Macalester College, St. Paul, Minnesota—National Merit Scholarships of at least $750; De Witt Wallace Distinguished Scholarships for National Merit Finalists or Commended with a B+ average for at least $750; De Witt Wallace Scholarships for middle-income students with good records; others.

University of Maine at Fort Kent, Fort Kent, Maine—Full-tuition scholarships to students accepted into their Honors Program: B average plus high SAT.

Manchester College, North Manchester, Indiana—One $400 scholarship: top 15 percent plus 1100 SAT or 25 ACT.

Marietta College, Marietta, Ohio—Presidential Scholarships worth $500 per year: automatic with 1100 SAT plus top tenth of class.

Mary Baldwin College, Staunton, Virginia—Fifty Rufus W. Bailey Scholarships worth $1,000 each per year: top 10 percent of class, 1200 SAT, plus Achievements of 650 or higher.

Mary Washington College, Fredericksburg, Virginia—Regional Scholarships for nonresidents of Virginia worth $1,000 per year; others for Virginia residents.

Marygrove College, Detroit, Michigan—Scholar Awards worth $1,000 or $500.

University of Maryland, College Park, Maryland—A small number of academic scholarships for students who enter Honors Program.

Mercyhurst College, Erie, Pennsylvania—Several Presidential Scholarships worth as much as full tuition: exam given on campus; $500 Honor Scholarships: students with strong records; Creative Arts and Athletic Scholarships.

Meredith College, Raleigh, North Carolina—Several scholarships including music and National Merit, worth $250 to $1,500 per year.

Messiah College, Grantham, Pennsylvania—Academic scholarships worth $250 to $750 per year: top 10 percent plus 1000 SAT or 22 ACT; Family Discount of $100 for each student if two or more from a family attend simultaneously; dependents of full-time, active ministers receive $150 discount.

University of Miami, Coral Gables, Florida—Full-tuition scholarships: top 5 percent plus 1300 SAT; $2,000 per year: top 10 percent plus 1200 SAT; also music scholarships.

Michigan State University, East Lansing, Michigan—Alumni Distinguished Scholarships worth $11,000 over four years plus any out-of-state tuition differential: by invitation only (invitations sent to best-qualified students who apply in the fall); also sponsors National Merit and National Achievement Scholars.

C. Misericordia, Dallas, Pennsylvania—Honor scholarships.

Monmouth College, West Long Branch, New Jersey—Faculty Merit Award worth $500 per semester: top 15 percent plus 1100+ SAT.

Moravian College, Bethlehem, Pennsylvania—Comenius Scholarships: $400 awarded without need, more with need.

Morgan State University, Baltimore, Maryland—One $1,000 a year scholarship.

Morris Harvey College, Charleston, West Virginia—Academic Scholarships worth $1,500 a year: valedictorians, salutatorians, and National Merit Finalists.

Mount Saint Mary's College, Emmitsburg, Maryland—Presidential Scholarships worth $1,000 to $1,500 per year.

College of Mount Saint Vincent, Riverdale, New York—Full-tuition and partial-tuition competitive scholarships.

Muskingam College, New Concord, Ohio—Automatic $500 per year to valedictorian; also $300 for outstanding performance in specific area such as music, art, debate.

Nasson College, Springvale, Maine—Thirty full-tuition scholarships, including twelve for athletics; academic scholarships: top fifth of class plus 1300 SAT or 700 in one half.

National College of Education, Evanston, Illinois—Competitive scholarships.

Nebraska Wesleyan, Lincoln, Nebraska—Wesleyan Scholarship worth $1,100 per year; also others.

Neumann College, Aston, Pennsylvania—Nine academic scholarships: one full tuition, four $1,200 per year, four $600 per year.

New England College, Henniker, New Hampshire—Scholarships worth $1,000 per year: top 15 percent plus good SAT; also small number of athletic scholarships for ice hockey and skiing.

New Mexico Institute of Mining and Technology, Socorro, New Mexico—Academic scholarships: B averages or better plus high ACT scores.

College of New Rochelle, New Rochelle, New York—President's, Academic, Honor, and Women's Leadership Scholarships (amounts of awards uncertain).

North Carolina Wesleyan College, Rocky Mount, North Carolina—Lamplighters Awards worth up to $1,000 per year: top third of class, 900 SAT, plus activities; also Dean's Award Scholarships worth up to full tuition: academics, leadership, or performing activities.

Northeastern Christian Junior College, Villanova, Pennsylvania—Academic, athletic, fine arts, and other scholarships, some worth as much as half tuition.

Northeastern University, Boston, Massachusetts—Thirty full-tuition Ell Scholarships for outstanding achievement.

Northern Illinois University, DeKalb, Illinois—University Scholarship worth $5,400 per year: top 10 percent plus 27 ACT.

The College of Notre Dame of Maryland, Baltimore, Maryland—Twenty Academic Achievement Awards worth $1,000 per year: top 15 percent of class and nominated by high school; also Equal Opportunity Scholarships for minority students worth $1,000 a year.

Oberlin College, Oberlin, Ohio—One $5,000 per year Dow Chemical Company Scholarship for chemistry major who plans to pursue a Ph.D. in chemistry.

Oglethorpe University, Atlanta, Georgia—Merit Scholarships worth $1,900: top 15 percent plus 1000 SAT or 23 ACT.

University of Oklahoma, Norman, Oklahoma—Scholarships worth $450 to $1,500 per year.

Ohio Wesleyan University, Delaware, Ohio—Wesleyan Scholarship worth $1,000 per year: top twentieth plus 1200 SAT or 30 ACT.

Old Dominion University, Norfolk, Virginia—Scholarships worth $750 per year: top 10 percent.

Oral Roberts University, Tulsa, Oklahoma—Academic scholarships.

Pacific Lutheran University, Tacoma, Washington—President's Scholarship worth $600 per year: top tenth plus 1000 SAT or 25 ACT.

Pfeiffer College, Misenkeimer, North Carolina—Academic and athletic scholarships.

Philadelphia College of Pharmacy and Science, Philadelphia, Pennsylvania—Twenty half-tuition scholarships based on science aptitude examination.

University of Pittsburgh, Pittsburgh, Pennsylvania—School of Engineering: two Dean's High Honor Scholarships worth $1,250 per year; six Honors Scholarships worth $600 per year; twenty Freshman Honor Scholarships worth $500, nonrenewable.

Point Park College, Pittsburgh, Pennsylvania—Full-tuition Faculty Scholarships; $1,000 per year Trustee Grants.

University of Puget Sound, Tacoma, Washington—Trustee Scholarship worth $1,500 per year: top quarter plus 1200 SAT.

Queens College, Charlotte, North Carolina—A large number of academic and leadership scholarships.

Quinnipiac College, Hamden, Connecticut—Twenty half-tuition scholarships per year: over 1200 SAT plus good grades.

Randolph-Macon College, Ashland, Virginia—Academic Scholarships worth from third to half tuition: top tenth plus 1200 SAT.

Randolph-Macon Woman's College, Lynchburg, Virginia—Distinguished Scholarships worth $1,250 per year; Given Scholarships worth $500 per year; Randolph-Macon

Award $500 nonrenewable; Math Award $500 nonrenewable; $750 per year deduction for the daughter of a minister.

University of the Redlands, Redlands, California—Talent scholarships worth $1,000 each per year.

Reed College, Portland, Oregon—Merit Awards worth $1,000 the first year and $500 each of the next three years.

Rensselaer Polytechnic Institute, Troy, New York—Alumni Scholarship worth $500 per year.

Rice University, Houston, Texas—National Merit and National Achievement Scholars are sponsored; more than a hundred scholarships per year: students automatically considered upon application to the university, top ten awards are full tuition.

University of Richmond, Richmond, Virginia—Several types of scholarships from $400 to $2,000 per year.

Roanoke College, Salem, Virginia—Bittle Scholarships worth $2,000 per year: want top tenth plus 1200 SAT.

University of Rochester, Rochester, New York—Fifty Alumni Regional Scholarships worth $500 minimum (nominated by Alumni Regional Committees); Joseph C. Wilson Scholarships worth $1,000 minimum; Bausch and Lomb Scholarships worth $500 minimum; Rochester Engineering Scholarships worth $500 minimum.

Rochester Institute of Technology, Rochester, New York—Several types of scholarships depending upon the major, from $500 to full tuition: campus competition.

Rollins College, Winter Park, Florida—Academic Achievement Scholarships worth $3,000 per year.

Roosevelt University, Chicago, Illinois—Academic scholarships from half to full tuition, also music awards through Chicago Musical College.

Saginaw Valley State College, University Center, Michigan—Many academic scholarships up to full tuition.

Saint Andrews Presbyterian College, Laurinburg, North Caro-

lina—Ten academic scholarships worth $2,000 each, fifteen worth $1,000 each.

Saint Francis College, Loretto, Pennsylvania—Academic scholarships worth $500 to $1,500 per year: top fifth plus good SAT.

Saint Joseph's College, Rensselaer, Indiana—Automatic half tuition scholarship: top ten percent plus 1100 or higher SAT; automatic quarter tuition: top 15 percent plus 1000 or higher SAT.

Saint Joseph's College, Philadelphia, Pennsylvania—Principal Scholarships (high school principals nominate students) worth $1,500 to $2,000 per year: top fifth plus 1200 SAT.

Saint Vincent College, Latrobe, Pennsylvania—Automatic $250 per year scholarship for an Eagle Scout; others worth up to $500 a year for leadership in school, community, or church groups.

Salem College, Winston-Salem, North Carolina—Lucy Hanes Chatham Awards worth $3,000 per year; also other awards worth $500 per year.

Seattle Pacific University, Seattle, Washington—Scholarships worth up to $1,000 per year.

Seattle University, Seattle, Washington—Honors Scholarship worth up to $1,200 per year: top fifth plus 1100 SAT.

Seton Hall University, South Orange, New Jersey—A number of Academic Scholarships worth up to $1,000 per year.

Shenandoah College and Conservatory of Music, Winchester, Virginia—Presidential Scholarship worth up to $2,500 per year: over 1100 SAT or 25 ACT; also music scholarships and hospital scholarships for nursing students.

Shippensburg College, Shippensburg, Pennsylvania—Full-tuition scholarships: top 10 percent plus 1200 SAT.

Sonoma State College, Sonoma, California—Full-tuition music and science scholarships.

University of South Carolina, Columbia, South Carolina—Carolina Scholarships worth $2,000 per year: must be from South Carolina and have 1200 SAT; Trustee Scholarships worth full tuition, President's Scholarships worth half tuition: can be from out-of-state, but competition is keen; Alumni Scholarships worth $500 per year: want 1200 SAT or top tenth.

Southampton College of Long Island University, Southampton, New York—Presidential Scholarships: substantial awards for 87 or better high-school average plus 1200 or better SAT.

University of Southern California, Los Angeles, California—Presidential Scholarships worth $500, nonrenewable: 3.95 GPA plus 1250 SAT or 27 ACT; also Trustee's Scholarships and Alumni Merit Awards worth $1,000 and $500 each.

Southern Illinois University, Carbondale and Edwardsville, Illinois—Full-tuition scholarships: top tenth and 28 ACT.

Spring Garden College, Chestnut Hill, Pennsylvania—Several $500-per-year scholarships: competitive exam.

Stephens College, Columbia, Missouri—Stephens Honors Scholarships worth up to full tuition: top 6 percent of class plus good SAT or ACT; National Merit Scholarships worth $1,000 per year.

Stetson University, DeLand, Florida—Four Landers Scholars awards per year worth $1,000 to $2,500 per year: 3.5 GPA plus 1200 SAT or 28 ACT.

Stevens Institute of Technology, Hoboken, New Jersey—Presidential Scholarship is worth $5,500 per year: top tenth plus 1200 SAT.

Swarthmore College, Swarthmore, Pennsylvania—Thomas B. McCabe Achievement Awards worth $6,200 a year: must be resident of Delaware County, Pennsylvania.

Sweet Briar College, Sweet Briar, Virginia—Ten scholarships per year worth $1,150 per year: want academic excellence plus contribution to school and community.

University of Tampa, Tampa, Florida—Merit Scholarships worth $500 to $2,000 per year: 3.5 GPA plus 1000 SAT; Performing Arts Scholarship worth $2,000 per year: 2.5 GPA plus outstanding ability in chorus, drama, band/orchestra, chamber ensemble, or jazz ensemble; also Creative Writing Scholarships.

Temple University, Philadelphia, Pennsylvania—Outstanding Achievement Scholarship worth full tuition for four years: nominated by high school, one per high school; also $400 music awards.

Texas A & M, College Station, Texas—President's Scholarship worth $1,500 per year: want top 25 percent plus 1100 SAT.

Texas Christian University, Fort Worth, Texas—Chancellor Scholarships worth $3,000 per year: top twentieth plus 1400 SAT; Dean's Scholarships worth $1,500 per year: top tenth plus 1300 SAT; Academic Achievement Awards worth $550 to $1,200 per year: top 15 percent plus 1100 SAT; National Merit Finalists who list TCU as a first choice have an excellent chance of being awarded TCU Merit Scholarships worth a minimum of $750 per year; other scholarships for valedictorians, musicians, and artists.

Thiel College, Greenville, Pennsylvania—Several kinds of honor scholarships worth from $200 to $1,000 per year; Clergy Grants of $600 per year: awarded to the dependents of clergymen; Family Grants: discount of $250 for a family if two are attending simultaneously.

Transylvania University, Lexington, Kentucky. Academic scholarships.

Trenton State College, Trenton, New Jersey. Alumni Scholarship worth $500 per year.

Tri-State University, Angola, Indiana. Merit Scholarships up to $1,000 per year.

Trinity University, San Antonio, Texas. Jesse H. Jones Scholarship for men and Mary Gibbs Scholarship for women: interest in public affairs.

Tulane University, New Orleans, Louisiana. Ten Dean's Honor Scholarships per year worth full tuition.

Union College, Barbourville, Kentucky. Scholarships worth $1,000 per year: top 3 percent of class; also, students over 900 on the SAT receive scholarships worth $500 to $1,000 (900 SAT = $500; 1150 SAT = $1,000).

Upsala College, East Orange, New Jersey. Honors scholarships worth $1,000 per year: top tenth plus 1100 SAT.

Ursinus College, Collegeville, Pennsylvania. Presidential Scholarships worth $200 to $700 per year: based largely on leadership talents; also one Gulf Honors Scholarship per year worth $1,500 per year.

University of Utah, Salt Lake City, Utah. Several scholarships; best is full tuition.

Valparaiso University, Valparaiso, Indiana. Academic and music awards worth up to $2,500 a year.

Vanderbilt University, Nashville, Tennessee. Several very competitive $5,000-per-year scholarships; also Grantland Rice Scholarship worth $21,500 over four years: awarded to an outstanding young sportswriter.

Villanova University, Villanova, Pennsylvania. Eight Presidential Scholarships worth full tuition for four years: top five in class and 1300 SAT (not necessary to apply; potential winners are contacted).

Virginia Polytechnic Institute, Blacksburg, Virginia. Hahn Engineering Scholarships worth full tuition first year, further awards possible in future years: top 10 percent of class or 1200 SAT plus 650 math or National Merit Semifinalist; also Pratt Scholarships toward engineering tuition and study-abroad programs; also Founder's Day Scholarships worth $500.

Virginia Wesleyan College, Virginia Beach, Virginia. Scholarships (amount uncertain): top fifth plus 1000 SAT.

Wake Forest University, Winston-Salem, North Carolina. Forty Guy T. Carswell Scholarships per year worth $1,500 per year (more possible with need) plus $1,000 toward a summer independent experience; also four Reynolds Scholarships worth about $30,000 over four years: want outstanding scholars and creative leadership.

Washington and Jefferson College, Washington, Pennsylvania. Ten Presidential Scholarships worth $500 to $2,000 per year: top tenth plus 1200 SAT.

Washington College, Chestertown, Maryland. Merit Scholar Awards worth $1,000 per year; also Sophie Kerr Gift in English Literature worth $1,000 per year: talent in English or American literature.

Washington University, St. Louis, Missouri. Thirty-eight scholarships worth full tuition plus $1,000 per year offered by College of Arts and Sciences, School of Engineering and Applied Science, and School of Business per year; School of Fine Arts offers two $5,000 scholarships per year.

Washington and Lee University, Lexington, Virginia. Forty Honor Scholarships worth $1,000 per year: top 10 percent plus 1200 SAT; also National Merit Scholarships.

Waynesburg College, Waynesburg, Pennsylvania. Two Outstanding Scholars Program awards per year, worth full tuition each year: top 1 percent of class, plus good SAT and recommendations; Presidential Honor Scholarship worth $1,000 per year: top tenth plus 1100 on SAT; Honor Scholarship worth $500 per year: top tenth or at least 1100 SAT.

Webb Institute of Naval Architecture, Glen Cove, New York. Full-tuition scholarships awarded to all accepted students.

Webster College, St. Louis, Missouri. Scholarships worth $200 to $1,200 per year.

Wells College, Aurora, New York. Three Henry Wells Scholarships worth $4,000 per year: top 5 percent plus 1300

SAT; also twenty Margaret Sessions Burke Scholarships worth $1,000 per year.

Wesley College, Dover, Delaware. Honor Scholarships worth up to $500 per year: top 20 percent; music scholarships worth $1,000 per year.

Wesleyan College, Macon, Georgia. Scholar Program awards worth $2,000 per year: top tenth plus 1000 SAT.

West Virginia University, Morgantown, West Virginia. Achievement Scholarships for which tuition, registration fees, and any nonresident fees are waived: top 10 percent plus high ACT.

West Virginia Wesleyan College, Buckhannon, West Virginia. Honor scholarships.

Western Illinois University, Macomb, Illinois. Talent scholarships: athletics, music, art, theater, and debating; academic scholarships: top 15 percent plus 28 or better ACT.

Western New England College, Springfield, Massachusetts. Scholarships worth 100 percent tuition.

Westminster College, New Wilmington, Pennsylvania. Ten Presidential Scholarships worth $3,000 per year, fifteen worth $1,500: top 10 percent plus 1200 SAT or 27 ACT.

Wheeling College, Wheeling, West Virginia. Presidential Scholarships worth $1,000 per year: automatic eligibility for top 20 percent of class plus 3.0 GPA and 1000 SAT; Laut Honor Scholarship worth full tuition: competition open to those with 3.5 GPA plus 1200 SAT.

Whittier College, Whittier, California. Forty-five merit scholarships for freshmen.

Widener College, Chester, Pennsylvania. A few band scholarships.

William Jewell College, Liberty, Missouri. Valedictorian Award worth $1,500 per year; Salutatorian Award worth $1,000 per year; awards of $200 to $800 per year: top 5 percent of class.

William Woods College, Fulton, Missouri. Six Dance Scholarships for modern and ballet worth $1,000 each per year.

Wittenberg University, Springfield, Ohio. Has twenty Scholar Awards worth $1,000 each per year plus others worth $500 per year.

College of Wooster, Wooster, Ohio. Freshman Scholar Awards worth $1,000 for one year only: scholars assist faculty.

Xavier University, Cincinnati, Ohio. Eight full-tuition Achievement Scholarships per year; also a number of Presidential Scholarships.

Yanton College, Yanton, South Dakota. Presidential Scholarship worth $1,200 per year; also others.

York College of Pennsylvania, York, Pennsylvania. Music scholarships through the Adam Kohler Family Scholarship Trust; also Presidential Department Scholarships worth $1,200 per year (one per department).

GLOSSARY

ALAS—Auxiliary Loans to Assist Students: see **PLUS**.

ACT—American College Testing: processes Family Financial Statements (FFS) to determine expected family contribution for student aid applicants. ACT also administers a test called the ACT.

APP—Advanced Placement Program: a CEEB program that allows a student to gain college credit while still in high school.

Award Letter—the detailed listing of financial aid awarded to the student sent from the college financial-aid office and containing the financial-aid package.

BEOG—Basic Educational Opportunity Grant: recently renamed Pell Grant in honor of R. I. Senator Claiborne Pell.

Campus-Based Aid Programs—(NDSL, CWSP, SEOG) funds provided by the federal government and awarded by the school financial-aid officer.

CEEB—College Entrance Examination Board: the testing service that administers the SAT, Achievement tests, and other tests.

CLEP—College Level Examination Program: a testing program of CEEB that allows students to receive college credit if they are able to pass college level examinations.

CSS—College Scholarship Service: processes Financial Aid Forms (FAF) to determine expected family contribution for student aid applicants.

CWSP—College Work Study Program: job funds paid to the student as earned in part-time on-campus or off-campus positions. These funds are awarded by the school aid administrator from campus-based funds.

Dependent Student—one who is considered by the federal definition to be dependent on parents.

EFC—Expected Family Contribution: this figure is determined by a formula and indicates how much of the family's financial resources should be available for educational expenses for the academic year. EFC includes parent contribution and student contribution.

EI—Eligibility Index: for Pell Grant, a number determined by the federal formula by which the aid administrator determines the amount of Pell Grant award. The EI appears on the SAR sent to the student by the federal government.

FFS—Family Financial Statement: the financial-aid application form provided by American College Testing.

FAF—Financial Aid Form: the financial-aid application form provided by College Scholarship Service.

Financial-Aid Package—the total amount of financial aid the student receives. The school's aid administrator notifies the student of the amount and sources of aid in the financial-aid award letter.

Financial-Aid Transcript—a record of financial aid received by the student at a previous school. The school to which the student transfers will require this document from the previous college.

Full-time Student—a student determined to be enrolled by the full-time standards of the school. At semester, trimester, or quarter hour schools this is usually 9 or 12 credit hours.

Grace Period—currently in most loan programs, a six-month period before the student borrower must begin repayment of a student loan following withdrawal or attendance below half-time status.

Grant—need-based aid that does not require repayment.

GSL/FISL—Guaranteed Student Loan or Federally Insured Student Loan: these 9 percent loans for students allow borrowing of up to $2,500 per academic year ($12,500 total in undergraduate study).

Half-time—at most schools this means at least six credit hours per term.

Independent Student—one who is considered by the federal government to be independent of parents.

Loan—aid that must be repaid.

NDSL—National Direct Student Loan (formerly National Defense Student Loan): loan funds currently at 5 percent interest, awarded based on need to aid applicants by school aid administrator from campus-based funds.

Need-based Aid—aid that is based on the financial need of the student.

Origination Fee—in the GSL/FISL program, a 5 percent charge collected by the bank from the student loan proceeds. This fee is designed to reduce the federal amount paid to the banks while the student is enrolled in school.

Pell Grant—a federal grant that must be applied for directly rather than through the school.

PLUS—Parent Loan for Undergraduate Students: this 14 percent loan for parents and graduate students allows borrowing of up to $3,000 per academic year with repayment beginning in sixty days.

PSAT/NMSQT—Preliminary Scholastic Aptitude Test/National Merit Scholarship Qualifying Test: a short form of the SAT that is used to prepare students for the SAT while it also determines which students may win scholarships through the National Merit Scholarship Corporation.

Promissory Note—the legal document in loan programs that binds the borrower to the repayment obligation of the specific loan program.

ROTC—Reserve Officers' Training Corps: a military program that allows college students to become officers in the military upon graduation.

SAI—Student Aid Index: a number determined by the federal formula by which the school aid administrator will determine campus-based and Pell Grant awards. The SAI appears on the SAR sent to the student by the federal government.

SAR—Student Aid Report: a report sent to the student by the federal government for the Pell Grant and all campus-based aid programs. The student should immediately take this report to the school aid administrator who will look up the Student Aid Index (SAI) to determine campus-based and Pell Grant award amounts.

Satisfactory Academic Progress—each school that takes part in federal student aid programs must establish written standards of academic progress. To receive federal aid, the student must meet the standards of the school.

SAT—Scholastic Aptitude Test: a test administered by CEEB.

Scholarship—an award that does not need to be repaid. A scholarship may or may not be need based.

Self-help Aid—loans that require repayment or work funds that are expected to be earned.

Statement of Educational Purpose—a document that the student recipient of federal aid must sign to agree to use the funds for education-related expenses.

SEOG—Supplemental Educational Opportunity Grant: grant funds based on need to aid applicants by the school aid administrator from campus-based funds.

Work-Study—aid that is paid to the student as it is earned; see **CWSP.**

BIBLIOGRAPHY

Barron's Profiles of American Colleges. Vols. 1, 2. Woodbury, N.Y.: Barron's Educational Series, 1980.

Bowen, Howard R. *The Costs Of Higher Education.* San Francisco: Jossey-Bass, 1980.

Cohen, Marjorie Adoff. *The Whole World Handbook.* 1981–82 ed. New York: E. P. Dutton.

The College Cost Book, 1981–82. New York: College Entrance Examination Board, 1981.

The College Handbook, 1981–82. New York: College Entrance Examination Board, 1981.

The Federal Role in Postsecondary Education. San Francisco: Jossey-Bass, 1975.

Fiske, Edward B. *Selective Guide to Colleges, 1982–83.* New York: Times Books, 1982.

Garraty, John A., Klemperer, Lily von, and Taylor, Cyril J. H. *The New Guide to Study Abroad, 1981–82.* New York: Harper and Row, 1981.

The Insider's Guide to the Colleges, 1981–82. New York: Berkley, 1981.

Keeslar, Oreon. *Financial Aids for Higher Education.* 10th ed. Dubuque, Iowa: William C. Brown, 1982.

Kohl, Kenneth A. and Kohl, Irene C. *Financing College Education.* Revised and updated ed. New York: Harper and Row, 1981.

Leider, Robert. *The A's and B's of Academic Scholarships.* 4th ed. (1981–83). Alexandria, Va.: Octameron, 1981.

Lovejoy, Clarence E. *Lovejoy's College Guide.* New York: Simon and Schuster, 1981.

Mayhew, Lewis B. *The Carnegie Commission on Higher Education.* San Francisco: Jossey-Bass, 1974.

Nyquist, Ewald B., Arbolino, Jack N., and Hawes, Gene R. *College Learning Anytime, Anywhere.* New York: Harcourt, Brace, Jovanovich, 1977.

Peterson's Annual Guide to Undergraduate Study, 1981. Princeton, N.J.: Peterson's Guides, 1980.

ALSO RECOMMENDED

THE BLACK STUDENT'S GUIDE TO COLLEGES
By The Students of Brown University
Edited by Barry Beckham
$15.95 cloth   ISBN: 0-525-93256-9
$7.95 paperback   ISBN: 0-525-93257-7

DROPPING BACK IN
How to Complete Your College Education Quickly and
Economically
By Miriam Hecht & Lillian Traub
$14.50 cloth   ISBN; 0-525-93229-1
$9.25 paperback   ISBN: 0-525-93228-3

HAPPIER BY DEGREES
By Pam Mendelsohn
$7.95 paperback   ISBN: 0-525-47621-0

HOW TO GET INTO LAW SCHOOL
Revised Edition
By Rennard Strickland
$4.95 paperback   ISBN: 0-8015-3767-3

HOW TO GET INTO MEDICAL SCHOOL
By Marvin Fogel & Mort Walker
$7.25 paperback   ISBN: 0-8015-1628-5

INSIDE THE LAW SCHOOLS
A Guide By Students For Students
By Sally Goldfarb
$9.25 paperback   ISBN: 0-525-93243-7

THE STUDENT GUIDE TO FELLOWSHIPS & INTERNSHIPS
By The Students of Amherst College
$15.95 cloth   ISBN: 0-525-93155-4
$7.95 paperback   ISBN: 0-525-93147-3

THE WHOLE WORLD HANDBOOK
A Guide to Study, Work and Travel Abroad
By the Council on International Educational Exchange
$5.75 paperback   ISBN: 0-525-93171-6